# JAILBREAK

## The Making and Breaking
## of our Invisible Prisons

### An IFS Informed Escape

# JAILBREAK

## THE MAKING AND BREAKING
## OF OUR INVISIBLE PRISONS

AN **IFS** INFORMED ESCAPE

ANGELA J. HUEBNER, PHD, LMFT

Library of Congress Control Number: 2021919039

Huebner, Angela. Author.
Title: Jailbreak: The Making and Breaking of Our Invisible Prisons. An IFS
    Informed Escape/ Angela Huebner.—1st ed.
Includes bibliographical references.
1. Self-Help.

ISBN: 978-0-578-98510-7 (paperback).

Printed in United States of America.

*For Regina and Samantha,*
*May you always find your freedom.*

# JAILBREAK

## THE MAKING AND BREAKING
## OF OUR INVISIBLE PRISONS

AN
# IFS
INFORMED
ESCAPE

# TABLE OF CONTENTS

# FOREWORD

I am writing this during the Pandemic which has been a hugely destructive event but, for many people, has created a pause that led them to reassess their lives. For example, polls have shown that a huge number of them are now questioning their career choice and are seriously considering not returning to their jobs and looking for more meaningful work or life goals. If you are one of those people, then this book comes at the perfect time.

Maybe you've heard the admonition, "Dance as if no one is watching!" This book by Angela Huebner offers to expand that to "Live as if no one is watching!"

To greater or lesser degrees, we are all constrained by the parts of us that worry about pleasing people, and: put their needs first, not ask them for much, show them you are clever, not outshine them, look appropriate or attractive, avoid humiliation, be perfect, etc. As Huebner says, and uses her own life to illustrate, your socialization sentenced you to life in inner prison. Your essence, the you that you would be if not for all these worries, is so constrained and contained by these vigilant inner guards that you may hardly know that person anymore.

Huebner offers a path to freedom that differs from most

other self-help books. She says, "What if I could show you a way to reconnect with the whole of who you are, in service to your highest purpose as you know it? What if I could help you break out of the invisible prison in which you have been living--the one that keeps you small and scared?"

How is it different? First, she knows what she's talking about because she has walked her talk—released herself from her own incarceration and tells that story in ways that will move and inspire you.

Second as a university professor for many years, she has intensely studied and taught how to do it. This book is a wealth of information about neuroscience, developmental psychology and attachment theory, and the sociology of change.

Third, she is a certified Internal Family Systems (IFS) therapist with many years of practice. Consequently, in contrast most self-help advice that views your inner prison guards (aka "the ego," conditioned mind, or internalized parental voices) as the problem that you should override or demonize in your jail break, she advocates learning about their histories and appreciating how hard they're working to keep you safe. IFS encourages you to befriend these protective parts, heal the vulnerable parts they protect and then help them all unload the extreme beliefs they got from family or cultural experiences, and bring them with you as you make your escape.

As you try out the concepts and practices in this book, you will not only sense the possibility of freedom, but you'll start on the path toward it. Ultimately, you'll be able to agree with Huebner's statement about herself: "I realized it was perfectly acceptable for me to meet my own needs and follow my own desires with no apologies. I was done living to ensure everyone's comfort but my own."

~Richard C. Schwartz, PhD, founder of Internal Family Systems Model (IFS)

# A NOTE ABOUT INTERNAL FAMILY SYSTEMS

If you go to my website (angelahuebner.com), you'll find this description:

I believe that when we are out of alignment with ourselves or with our partners, our system—our body, our mind, our spirit—lets us know. Sometimes our system uses the language of depression. Sometimes worry and anxiety. Sometimes anger or sadness. Sometimes aches and pains. Our internal system provides us feedback if we listen. Every behavior, belief, or symptom makes perfect sense when we slow down long enough to understand it. From a developmental perspective, at one point in time, this way of being was the best or only option for our survival. If it weren't, we wouldn't have used it for so long. Sometimes, however, our behaviors, beliefs, and symptoms no longer serve us. I work to help you realign to a way of being that works in current time. I help you get unstuck.

This is Internal Family Systems (IFS).

IFS therapy is an evidence-based, non-pathologizing psychotherapy practice developed by Dr. Richard Schwartz in the 1980s. It's truly a revolutionary take on thinking about and working with our internal world. It is built on several core assumptions.

First, IFS assumes that we are inherently good and that we all have an innate ability to heal. For me, having been raised Lutheran (a branch of Protestant Christianity), the idea of inherent goodness flew in the face of the "confession" I recited alongside my family every Sunday morning: "I admit that I am by nature sinful and unclean..." The idea that I might not be bad got my attention.

Second, IFS normalizes the idea of multiplicity of mind. It assumes we all have multiple parts of ourselves—we are not monolithic. One part can be angry, while another is sad. A part can be excited even while another is anxious. Rather than seeing this multiplicity as pathological, IFS believes it is a normal way of being. This idea helped me get out of the trap of trying to figure out which thought, feeling, or belief I was having was "right" when they were often contradictory.

Finally, IFS assumes that we get out of balance when our parts take on burdens, defined as extreme beliefs, emotions, and responses. These burdens accumulate from confusing or traumatic interactions with others. These burdens can compel our parts to move into survival mode, cutting us off from our basic goodness and growth. This idea helped me have compassion for the parts of myself that I hated. It helped me see a path for healing.

Based on these assumptions, Dr. Schwartz developed a specific way of working with clients and their internal worlds to bring their systems back into balance. Jailbreak is informed by the assumptions and practices of the IFS model.

For more information about IFS, go to www.ifs-institute.com

-AH

# INTRODUCTION

"The worst thing that could happen to you, Angela, is nothing." Those words, spoken by my spiritual teacher, Sonia Choquette, cut me to the core. I was talking with her about my sense of loneliness in my life--my feeling of being stuck on the outside looking in. Despite my active and seemingly successful life, I felt empty and alone. It was never enough. I was never enough. Sonia's statement didn't mean that nothing bad was ever going to happen to me. What she meant was that it would be a shame if I never allowed myself to fully show up in the world as me. She helped me realize that my fear of getting life "wrong" was cutting me off from true connection and actually living. My fear was imprisoning me. She reminded me that true connection is possible only when we are clear about who we are.

Through our conversations, I realized that I had I spent so many years trying to be who I thought others wanted me to be that I forgot to pay attention to who I actually am. I was living under the assumption that others knew more about what was right for me than I did. I believed that if I just got it right—translated, if I just did what others expected—my happily ever after was guaranteed. Sonia's comment woke me up to the fact that this strategy for running my life was no longer working. She woke me up to the fact that I needed to actively decide how I wanted to live today; that charting my course based on its convenience to others was contributing to the long, slow death of my spirit. In short, she helped to wake me up to the fact that I was responsible for both defining and living my own "happily ever after." It's all you kid.

What if I could show you a way to reconnect with the whole of who you are, in service to your highest purpose as you know it? What if I could help you break out of the invisible prison in which you have been living--the one that keeps you small and scared? I have been in the mental health field for 30 years--as a professor, a researcher, and a clinician. I hold a Ph.D. in human development and am a licensed marriage and family therapist.

What I have noticed in my work is that at the very core of most mental health issues is a deep longing for connection. We want to be seen and understood. We need to feel valued. All the "symptoms" that bring people to my office are really just adaptive strategies, protectors of our hearts, designed to help us get connection or to numb us from the pain of not having it. These maladies happen when we think we are in it alone. They are a side effect of disconnection. Indeed, study after study confirms that loneliness, another word for disconnected, is correlated with heart disease, high blood pressure, sleep disorders, substance use, depression, anxiety, and a host of other mental health problems.[1] Symptoms aren't the enemy—they are the markers of disconnection.

I wrote this book to share a glimpse of what I have learned on this journey to freedom and to invite you to come out of the darkness of the internal prison in which you may be caught. It describes the process I have learned and refined over the years in my practice as a psychotherapist, university professor, and full-time spiritual seeker. It's what I have found in my personal work and what I do with my clients and in my workshops. It's my profession and my passion. The tools are an amalgamation of what I have been drawn to over the past three decades. This includes an understanding of our neurobiology (our "hardwiring" for connection), developmental psychology (how we "learn" to connect), and psychotherapy (tools for helping us reconnect). The ideas presented here are anchored in stories of my own incarceration and escape as well as composite case studies of my clients (identifying information has been changed to protect confidentiality).

By way of introduction, I want to share my story to illustrate how innocently incarceration can start. Let me begin by acknowledging that I know I was loved in my family. That's important to remember because, as you will see, love and imprisonment aren't mutually exclusive. I learned through experience in my family that being perfect, needing nothing, and accommodating everyone was the key to connection. If I was perfect, I didn't need anything. If I didn't need anything, I wasn't inconvenient. If I met everyone else's needs, I was valuable. I learned to be a giver rather than a taker. I thought this was the price of belonging. I was taught that my value depended upon what I could do, how I performed, and how I appeared. I thought more perfection and pleasing would translate into less aloneness.

Of course they didn't. Instead, these strategies kept me in solitary confinement even though I was surrounded by people. I was so focused on seeing others and figuring out what they needed that I didn't let them see me. Over time, I lost track of me too. I realize now that I was caught in a kind of prison of my own making, built by a losing strategy of how I thought I was supposed to be in the world. It was time for a change. But how did I get locked up in the first place? Let me explain…

I grew up in rural Nebraska, in a middle-class family that did well financially but was bankrupt when it came to emotional intimacy—emotional connection. Intellect and cleverness were the currency of our family. Sarcasm was the language of choice. These could buy us temporary approval and a sense of belonging. Emotions did not. Serious conversations were discouraged. No real discussion of politics, no questioning of our religion, and no discussion of fear, anxiety or sadness. These topics might get uncomfortable. These were the family rules.

My father was a solid role model in this regard. He was the town's dentist, well respected and good at his craft. He was organized and successful; a leader in the community. When he wasn't working or volunteering, he loved nothing more than organizing the tools in his garage and developing more efficient ways of doing things. He painted lines on the floor in the garage between which my brother and I were to park our bikes ("to maximize room in the garage", he said), and developed an automatic watering system for the flowers in the backyard ("because I can"). At one point he froze milk in ice cube trays ("because each cube is exactly a quarter of a cup and it's great for cooking!"). These are just a few examples of his inventiveness. He was clever.

He was also skilled at avoiding any conversation or situation that might get emotionally intense. He was, and still is, the master of avoiding hard emotions. His emotional void left my mother incredibly lonely. She felt out of place in the small town to which they moved after he finished dental school. My father's busyness left my mother to figure it out on her own. Not surprisingly, my mother was depressed. She tried to kill herself when I was five.

It was late in the summer of 1972. I can still remember hearing sharp words between my parents followed by the slamming of their bedroom door. This was remarkable because there were never any sharp words or slamming of doors in our house. I was used to the occasional tense silence but never tense words and certainly not slamming doors. At least not from my parents. This caught my attention. Within the month, and with no explanation, I found myself in a new city, a new school, and a new house with my mother and brother, 250 miles away from the place I had called home. My parent's separation had begun.

It was short. My parents reunited within the same year. For

me as a developing five-year-old, however, that year left a mark. I was thrown into a whole new routine in a whole new city and a whole new school. It was overwhelming. I was expected to walk home on my own after school because my mother had to work (my brother was older and in a different school). My mother was counting on me to take care of myself, at least for a few hours. I blew it on the very first day. Did I mention I was five? Nothing looked familiar on my walk to my "new" home. I sat down on the curb and tried not to cry. I was certain my mother was going to be upset with me for not being able to get myself home. How could I be so stupid? The tears that finally came were from frustration and fear of her disappointment. It never occurred to me to worry about my own safety or to ask for help. It seems that at the tender age of five, I had already learned to be ashamed of not knowing, ashamed of my imperfection.

At the time, I thought nobody cared about what I thought about the move or how the transition was going for me. My mother certainly didn't ask, and my father was predictably silent on the topic. The story I told myself was that I was a burden for her to manage as she tried to figure out her new life. I adapted so that I took up as little space as possible. I didn't want anyone to figure out that I didn't know what I was doing. I didn't want to be abandoned, which I was sure would happen given that my parents split after what appeared to me to be one minor spat. Of course the separation was more complicated than that, but at the time I was unaware. "Fighting is bad"—that was the best explanation my five-year-old brain could come up with. I was quite convincing to myself. A connection between conflict and abandonment was seared into my brain. The foundation of my prison was being poured.

When we returned home to live with my father, we all pretended everything was fine. My parents' separation became The Event Never to Be Spoken Of, forever hidden from understanding. I think they assumed that we were too young to remember. Life went on and we doubled down on appearing to be the perfect family. My father played the organ at church, was a volunteer fireman, and served on the city council. My brother and I sang duets. My mother kept the perfect house and had dinner on the table every evening at 5:30 pm sharp. We spent weekends on the lake, swimming, waterskiing, and fishing. Pretty picture. The strategy seemed to be that if the outside looks good, nobody will question the inside. Maybe it won't be up for judgment. I played along.

Looking back, I see that this period of my life was pivotal in forming my belief that perfection and pleasing were the way to go. Behind that pretty picture was a quiet mess. I had a mother who was depressed. I had a father who was anxious. I also had an older brother with attention deficit disorder (ADD), which in the 1970s wasn't yet classified as a mental health disorder. After college, he came out as gay. As you can imagine, all these factors created an interesting family dynamic.

My mother tried hard to keep things predictable so as not

to upset my father. She seemed to anticipate his every need and acquiesce to all his preferences. It was as though she were in charge of managing his anxiety. Her needs didn't seem to count. My brother, as you might imagine, was anything but predictable. This didn't bode well for his relationship with my father. From an early age, I watched their sparring, which continued well into his college years. When my father wasn't working, he either checked out on the couch or puttered around in the garage with one of his many projects. My mother spent her days in the basement with soap operas and laundry. She never left the house without perfect makeup and a perfectly color-coordinated outfit.

As for me, I retreated into books and extracurricular activities. I learned to go above and beyond what was expected of me. I truly believed that if I worked hard enough, and did it "right" enough, I could prove to myself (and those around me) that there was nothing wrong with me. That I was worthy of belonging. So I studied harder. I got stellar grades. I was an excellent athlete. I looked pretty.

It didn't work.

So I did it more.

To be clear, I don't think that my experiences were particularly unique. I share them with you here because I recognize that these experiences set the stage for what I came to believe about myself. It framed the way I learned to show up in the world. I learned to be perfect without drawing too much attention to myself. I learned to be pleasing but not provocative. I learned to avoid any topic that might be remotely controversial. I rarely said what I truly thought. And, perhaps most importantly, I learned not to do anything that might embarrass my family. A true midwesterner.

And so it began for me as it begins for all of us. Now I look back and think: What was happening in my brain? In my bones? What was getting coded in my DNA—my view of myself and my place in the world? Let's review. The people who loved me the most also gave me the message that I only counted when I was perfect and pleasing, when I didn't question or create a fuss. When I made them look good. No scandals.

The construction of my jail began with the adoption of my first strategy for adapting in my family: Perfection. The sarcasm hurled at me for any mistake stung. I was determined to get it right. My perfectionistic tendencies were over the top. I remember arguing with my middle school science teacher about one point on an exam. One point! I had earned a 99% but that wasn't good enough. (Sorry Mr. C.!).

I also became the poster child for self-sufficiency. "Needs? What needs? I am fine. Don't worry about me." I learned that if I didn't admit needs, I wouldn't be disappointed when they weren't met, or worse, shamed for even having them. To be clear, figuring things out on one's own and being disciplined and organized are wonderful skills for life. The skills aren't the issue. It's the motivation under the behavior that builds the prison. My perfection was fueled by fear of abandonment, not by an innate love of learning. I believed my achievements were the only indicator of my worth. I thought achievement was the only way to get the connection that I craved—security against abandonment.

Of course it wasn't. Turns out perfection and self-sufficiency have some downsides. For starters, I never allowed myself to be truly vulnerable with others. Instead, I showed them only what I thought they wanted to see, not who I really was. I truly believed they would only accept the polished version of me—not the messy one. This meant I was monitoring others' reactions all the time. Adjusting my response. Keeping them comfortable. I was always on the lookout for the next "right" step, then working like crazy to achieve it. I usually succeeded. Failure was not an option in my code of survival.

On the upside, on paper, (and on Facebook!) I was a clear success. Cliff notes version: I graduated at the top of my high school class. I attended college on an academic scholarship and graduated Phi Beta Kappa. I went to graduate school, intent on studying human behavior. I landed a job in academia and became a tenured university professor. I secured millions of dollars in grants and contracts through my research on military families. I was on Anderson Cooper (for five seconds, but still...!), and quoted in Newsweek Magazine. My studies were cited in Congressional testimony, and I was published in peer-reviewed journals. I was at the top of my game as far as the university was concerned. My personal life was equally impressive. I had circle of interesting friends. I married a wonderful man. We bought a house and had two children. The dog came a few years later. We paid our bills, saved for the girls' college and our retirements. We even managed some fantastic vacations.

Looking back, I actually think I did have the approval and connection I was so desperate to receive, but I couldn't allow myself to believe it was true. I couldn't allow myself to take it in. I couldn't let myself relax into my belonging because I feared it was fleeting. I should have been over the moon, but I wasn't. I still felt something was lacking. Recently, I ran into one of my former graduate students who said, "You've got to know, Angela, that all of us wanted to be you when we grew up!" That never occurred to me. I didn't see myself as a role model. I assumed I was invisible. It seems the very strategies I used to chase inclusion actually kept me in solitary confinement. I just didn't know it. The prison created precisely what it was designed to avoid.

Eventually, a cool thing happened. Well, first a series of really bad things happened. Over time, the people who said they loved me the most--the ones I had tried so hard to fit in with, the ones I tried to please--disappointed me the most. When I was just 30 years old, my mother died after a short bout with cancer. She didn't even try to fight it. To this day, I am not sure if she knew it was futile or if it was just her way of completing her own escape. In his grief, my father told me it would have been easier for him if I had died rather than her.

In hindsight, I think he was trying to explain his pain, but I didn't take it well. It didn't help that he seemed to have no empathy for me as a motherless daughter. He remarried a year later. We became distant. A few years later, I suffered a miscarriage and felt like a failure. I had a falling out at my church. My husband hurt me deeply. This combination of experiences finally knocked me out of the fantasy that if I did the right thing, got the good grades, played by the rules, was pleasing, and didn't rock the boat, I would be rewarded. It wasn't happening.

I felt the fight growing between the part of me that wanted to play it safe and the part that wanted something more. I realized that no amount of perfection, achievement, or self-sufficiency was enough to guarantee me anything from anyone else. I eventually concluded the whole quest was ridiculous. I was finally, FINALLY sick of it. I was ready to break free. But how?

I got to work. I finally started really thinking about what I wanted. I started combining the science of the brain and mental health with metaphysical and spiritual concepts. I was drawing the blueprint for escape. Brick by brick, I began to break out of my internal jail. My first new tool was meditation, introduced to me by one of my dear friends and colleagues, Eric McCollum. Then I dug deep into a therapy model called "Internal Family Systems" (IFS) with Dick Schwartz. It was a game changer for me, and I devoured it with a hunger I hadn't known before. I dipped into Buddhism, including a stay at the Barre Center for Buddhist Studies, silent retreats with Tara Brach, LifeForce Yoga with Amy Weintraub, and of course Sixth Sensory Living with Sonia Choquette. I found an amazing therapist and got serious about yoga. All these remarkable people influenced how I crafted the blueprint for my escape—the one you hold in your hand.

I finally allowed myself to stop thinking about how everyone else would evaluate my choices and tuned fully into how I evaluated them. My metric became, "How does this feel in my gut?" rather than "How will this look on my resume?" From this position, I starting saying "No" to projects that didn't feel right and promotions that I didn't want. I learned to withstand other people's head-shaking and admonitions about what they considered to be my poor choices. I stopped explaining. I simply didn't feel the need to justify myself.

From a professional standpoint, I realized it was time to leave my tenured (translated: secure) position at the university. I had been there for nearly 17 years! While I had enjoyed the experience immensely, I began to realize that no matter how successful I was, it never felt like it was enough. *You got a grant? Great, when's the next one? You published three papers? Great—where's the book? You got great teaching reviews? Cool—now put all your classes online. You presented at a conference? Wonderful, when are you going to chair it?* I was exhausted.

I finally walked away from the university job that had defined me. The one that armored me with the appearance of intellect and, as learned in my family, worth. I walked away from tenure and its benefits, retirement income and titles. I walked away from what everyone expected me to do. I was done waiting for someone to come to my rescue. I realized it was perfectly acceptable for me to meet my own needs and follow my own desires with no apologies. I was done living for everyone's comfort but my own. Done. I opened my own full-time private psychotherapy practice. It was thriving within the first year. I loved it.

Jailbreak invites you into your own journey of change. Each chapter introduces the concepts that I teach my clients and students as well as stories that illustrate their application. Each chapter also has a behind the scenes brain science explanation for how the process of incarceration and freedom are unfolding. Don't worry, the science is presented in a humorous and accessible language, honed by years of conversations and explanations with both my students and clients. "Your Turn" exercises, opportunities for exploration and application to your own life, are scattered throughout the chapters. A chance for "Extra Credit" appears at the end of most chapters. I recommend you read the book with a journal close at hand to track your experiences.

Chapter 1, Foundations, introduces three fundamental processes of human development—attachment, attunement, and emotional regulation. These processes are critical for early connection to caregivers and thus infant survival in the world. Our connection, or lack thereof, sets the stage for subsequent development and functioning.

Chapter 2, Getting Stuck, explores how the blueprint of our prisons are drawn. It explores the connection between learning, memory pattern matching, and subsequent beliefs and behaviors. It also introduces the inmates and guards of our internal prison.

Chapter 3, Finding the Key, reveals the importance of the heart and how it houses the key to our jailbreak. It explores practices that facilitate connection to the key for the ensuing Jailbreak.

Chapter 4, Breaking Out, explores the stages of change and introduces specific practices to begin your journey out. This includes gaining the Guards trust and their permission to heal the prisoner(s).

Chapter 5, Staying Out, explores how to cultivate a vision for moving forward in our freedom. It reminds us that rather than trying to inoculate ourselves from future incarceration, the goal of this work is to get really good at the process of breaking out so that if and when we do get stuck again, we can relax into knowing the route to escape. Let the journey begin!

## CLASS IS IN SESSION.

## ♟ YOUR JAILBREAK

Get out your notebook because it's time to break it in. Take a few minutes to think about why you picked up this book.

Where in your life do you feel stuck?

_____

_____

_____

_____

_____

What do you want to stop thinking, feeling, or doing?

_____

_____

_____

_____

_____

If you could break out of these stuck patterns, what would you be thinking, feeling, and doing instead?

_____

_____

_____

_____

_____

## CHAPTER 1

# FOUNDATIONS

Evan rolled his eyes and let out a heavy sigh. "Are we seriously going to talk about my childhood?" he asked. "Indeed we are," I responded with a smile. "But the past is the past," he shot back. "It can't be changed so what's the point of dredging up all that crap? It's over," he said, as he sat back in his chair and folded his arms across his chest. Evan is certainly not the first client who is hesitant to revisit the past. He's also not the only one to honestly believe there is no connection between childhood experiences and present-day functioning.

In this chapter, I share with you what I shared with him. To understand how we are stuck today, we have to go back to the beginning to see how our jail cell was formed in the first place. When we understand how it was formed, we begin to shape the blueprint for escape. To this end, I teach my clients a bit about normative human development.

More specifically, I help them, (and now you!) understand how our early interactions form the foundation for how we view ourselves, how we learn to regulate our emotions, and how we learn to interact with the world. I draw upon the long-standing science of attachment, attunement, emotion, and emotional regulation. I also include recent findings from the Adverse Child Experiences Study that unequivocally demonstrate a connection between early childhood experiences and mental and physical health outcomes in adulthood. This is the Professor Huebner portion of the book. Class is in session (it's an easy A, I promise!).

## FIRST CONNECTIONS

The nature of our first attachment sets the initial stage for our development—both in terms of how we view ourselves and how we view others. From the moment of conception, we are attached to our mother. We are totally dependent upon her for protection and nourishment as we float along in the cocoon of her uterus. How the mother takes care of herself, what she eats, and how she feels all influence the unborn child. In fact, research reveals a direct connection between the mother's mental health (e.g. anxiety and depression) and the in utero development of the baby's hypothalamus-pituitary-adrenal axis (HPA)--the stress response portion of the brain. Other studies demonstrate a correlation between the mother's level of stress and the baby's in utero heartrate (another measure of stress), which persists even after delivery.[1]

Even after birth, when the literal cord has been cut, we remain dependent on our caretakers. We need more time for our brain and body to develop outside the womb. Some describes the first year of life as the second phase of gestation or "exterogestation."[2] This makes sense because we, unlike other mammals, aren't ready to hit the ground running upon arrival. Giving birth to a seven-pound baby is hard enough! I can't even begin to imagine what it would be like to deliver one the size of a toddler. Eeeeeek! It's readily apparent that babies change more in the first three years of life than at any other stage of development (puberty being the close second). Steady improvements in motor skills and independence unfold before our eyes. Similar steady changes are happening in the brain.

Scientists believe our brains have gone through various stages of evolution over time to get to their current state. Neuroscientist Dr. Paul MacLean proposed the "triune brain" theory back in the 1960s.[3] Although highly simplified, this model provides a great overview of our brain. Specifically, MacLean suggests there are three distinct brains, each with remnants of different levels of our species evolution. Why does this matter? Because understanding how your brain works is the first step to finding freedom.

So what are these three distinct brains? They include the brainstem, the limbic system, and the neocortex. While they are connected, that is to say they speak to each other, they also have primary responsibility for different aspects of our survival. Furthermore, different strategies of survival seem to be generated depending on which "brain" is in control in any given moment. They develop sequentially, starting from the bottom (i.e. brainstem) to the top (i.e. neocortex). According to this theory, our access to conscious thought was the last to evolve and occurred as our brains got bigger.

Developmentally, the brainstem is functional first and plays a large role in controlling our autonomic nervous system (ANS), which takes care of breathing, heart rate, blood flow, digestion, and elimination. All the good stuff that keeps our body functioning. It operates mostly outside of our conscious awareness on autopilot, without input from our thinking brain. It develops prenatally. Given its location above the spinal cord, it can send signals down to the body much more quickly than it can up to the neocortex—the thinking parts of the brain. In other words, the brainstem via the ANS can signal your body to react before your thinking brain has had a chance to interpret what just happened. The automatic nature of this function is imperative for our survival. Here's an example from my less-than-graceful life to illustrate.

Despite my parents' insistence of ballet classes from an early age, I still have the occasional stumble (sidenote: Can you even imagine how much worse it might be if I *hadn't* had all those classes?). In those moments, especially on a flight of steps, I find that as soon as my foot slips, the rest of my body instantly reacts in an attempt to keep me upright. My arms fly out to the side, my quadricep muscles engage, and my other foot adjusts. All this movement is finished and *then* my brain registers, "Oh man, I just about fell down the steps (again)." At this point, however, I am already safe and recovered, and the commentary about my gracefulness is simply commentary rather than instruction. In other words, I didn't say to myself in conscious awareness while I was falling, "Oh my, I have lost my balance, I should put my arms out to steady me, I should engage my quads, and my other foot should catch up." This would have taken too long and I would have found myself in a heap at the bottom of the stairs. The ANS is a big deal.

The second brain, the limbic system, is also functional at birth. It, too, is closely linked to our ANS. The limbic brain is also found in other mammals. At a very basic level, the limbic brain houses our emotional responses. Emotions can be thought of as messengers of the ANS. Researchers suggest that emotions arise from particular bio-chemicals in the body known as peptides.[4] These peptides create changes in our internal biology, organizing a behavioral response.

Based on input from the nervous system, emotions function to move us toward rewarding stimuli (e.g., latching on for mother's milk), or away from those that are threatening (e.g. startle reflex with loud noises). So for babies, the brainstem and limbic brain work together, automatically coordinating their bodily functions, signaling their needs to those around them. Because they don't yet have access to spoken language and aren't yet able to meet their own needs, infants rely on this language of emotion to signal the caregivers around them. At least five emotions are evident at birth: interest (eye gaze), enjoyment (smiling), anger and pain (crying), and disgust (cringe or pull away).[5] If they are paying attention, parents read these emotions and respond appropriately to meet their infant's needs in a timely fashion.

Conscious thought emerges when the third brain, the neocortex, begins to develop. This starts around age three but is not complete until our mid-twenties. Language, logic, and decision making all come from this third brain, more specifically, the prefrontal cortex part of the neocortex. Based on interpretation of bodily sensations (from the brainstem) and emotions (from the limbic system), the prefrontal cortex weaves together a story about our experience.

It is important to note that the sophistication of the "story" we create changes as we develop. Jean Piaget proposed that children go through four distinct phases of cognitive development.[6] A brief description of each shows the interplay between development and explanatory story. In the first stage, sensorimotor (ages 0-2), meaning is made via senses, tasting, touching, and observing. The second stage (ages 2-7), is referred to as preoperational. In this stage, children are egocentric, not yet able to take the perspective of others. This means that during these formative years, children are much more likely to see things as their fault. Their limited cognitive development makes it difficult for them to see situations as outside of their influence.

The third stage (ages 7-12) is called concrete operational. During this developmental period, children are becoming increasingly logical and organized in their thought. They still tend to adhere to "concrete" or black and white thinking. The final stage of cognitive development (ages 12+) is known as formal operational. Thoughts become more abstract and complex.

This story or the meaning we make of what we are feeling is a potent driver of our behavioral response, whatever our age. For example, last summer I was outside watching my daughter's softball game (she's quite good!). I was startled when something hit me on the head. It wasn't a hard hit—it just got my attention. I immediately looked around to see where it had come from. Looking up, I noticed a tree with a squirrel running around on its branches. The story my brain created was that an acorn hit my head because the squirrel knocked it off. I shrugged off the hit and returned my focus to the game. My girl was up to bat. My friend, however, was livid. "Did you see that kid throw that acorn at you?" she said, pointing across the bleachers.

My anger was ignited. How dare he! I looked around again, this time ready for a fight or at least a stern lecture. Same hit. Very different reaction. What changed? The meaning I made of the situation. When I thought the acorn was an accident, I let it go. My nervous system was calm. When I thought it was thrown at me on purpose, I got angry, my limbic system dumped the stress hormones needed to ready me for action—fists clenched and jaw set. Interpretation, a function of the prefrontal cortex portion of the neocortex, changes everything. This idea of meaning making is important, and we will return to throughout the book.

## ATTUNEMENT

Survival and growth depend on more than just food and shelter. A level of attuned interaction with our parents (or other consistent caregivers) is also necessary to promote optimal growth. "Attuned" simply means that the parent reads and responds appropriately to the child's emotional signals. In the process of paying attention to facial expressions, tone of voice, and body language, an attuned parent forms hypotheses (educated guesses) about what the child is feeling and needing.

These hypotheses guide the parental response. This might mean, for example, they recognize the child's cries of hunger and provide food. They may see that the child is frightened and provide comfort. They might realize the child is getting angry and intervene to calm him down. They might see the child is grumpy and realize he needs a nap. In other words, attuned parents read and respond. How do caregivers learn to attune?

It turns out, parts of our brain are wired to pick up the intentions of others. Mother Nature worked that into our physiology as a survival mechanism. Stephen Porges, a prominent neuroscientist, talks about social interactions and emotions as biobehavioral processes, an interaction between the social experience and our behavioral and emotional responses. Two parts of our nervous system in particular support this function.[7] The first are specialized neurons, called "mirror" neurons. Researchers in Italy stumbled onto them by accident as they were studying monkeys.[8]

These function as an internal "mirror," helping us understand others' emotional state and intended action. Mirror neurons are why both yawning and laughter are contagious. They are why we can get so involved in a movie that we "share" the actors' emotions. For example, as a professor, when I taught my students about mirror neurons, I began by showing a 5-minute clip from the movie "The Champ." I chose this clip (even though the vast majority of my students had never seen this movie circa 1979), because a Google search revealed it to be "the saddest movie scene ever" (true story!). The emotional scene between the dying boxer and the young boy is real tear jerker. Within minutes of viewing, most of my students had lumps in their throats and tears in their eyes. Why? Because they were attuned to the emotions of the gifted actors. Mirror neurons.

The vagus nerve is the second structure that supports survival. For those of you with a future on Jeopardy, the vagus nerve is the 10th cranial nerve, and it winds its way from the head (eyes, mouth, throat) all the way down to our visceral organs (heart, lungs, stomach, intestines). It is the only cranial nerve that extends down into the body. It serves as major information superhighway between our bodies and our brains. It is part of our parasympathetic nervous system—the brakes, or slow down portion of our response.

The vagus nerve actually promotes two types of slowing down. The first is relaxation and openness to connection with others (the ventral or "smart" vagus). This kicks in when we feel safe. The second slow down function is activated under extreme stress—when the option to fight or flee (from the gas pedal of the sympathetic nervous system) isn't possible. In these moments, the dorsal vagus nerve puts us into a freeze response, rendering us invisible, or giving the appearance of death (this is what is happening when possums "play" dead).

Porges's work reveals that the body is sending just as many signals to the brain as the brain is to the body, a reminder of the intricate connection between our physiological and emotional states, and the sympathetic and parasympathetic nervous systems. Our physiology can prompt a particular mood, just as a mood can prompt a particular physiological response. How does it work in action?

It was after 9:30 pm on a Tuesday night. I had just locked up the office, having finished teaching my evening class. I headed out into the dark parking lot, reaching into my bag for my keys. I was startled by the sound of breaking glass. As I looked up, I found myself caught in the cold stare of a young man standing next to a car, with its side window shattered. I froze. The hair on the back of my neck stood at attention. It felt like time stood still as we stared at each other. Suddenly, the man sprinted off, disappearing into the bushes, probably down to the public transit hub nearby. My hands shook as I unlocked my car and climbed inside, quickly relocking the door. I took a deep breath (okay, I actually took several). It was only then I remembered the reports of car vandalism and break-ins in the area. I was relieved to be safe.

What had just happened? Let's rewind. The novel sound caused me to look up. The impulse to freeze came from perceiving the man's ill intent. My body reacted in the way it needed to keep me safe—it froze, then when the threat was distracted, my body sought safety. My sympathetic and parasympathetic nervous systems functioned just as they should have to keep me safe. They detected threat and readied my body to respond with the fight, flight, or freeze response (or in some cases a combination of all three!). In this example, my body reacted first. Only when safety was restored did my prefrontal cortex make meaning of what had happened.

Remember, the vagus nerve flows information both directions—from the mind to the body and from the body to the mind. My parking lot experience was an example of the latter. For an example, of the former (mind to body), just think about your last flu shot experience. Did you focus on the needle (this is going to hurt!) or did you focus on the meaning of the injection (I'm not going get sick this flu season)? Your point of focus and meaning (pain or prevention) is a clear indicator of whether you tensed up your arm (bracing against "danger"/pain) or your relaxed it (inviting the antidote). This physiological response, tension or relaxation, in turn influenced the experience of the needle prick—was it "Ouch!" or "You're done already?!"

## EMOTIONAL REGULATION AND THE WINDOW OF TOLERANCE

As you can imagine, in my work with clients, emotional regulation is a big deal. But what does "emotional regulation" actually mean? Emotions are hardwired into our nervous system as part of our survival strategy. They serve to organize our behavioral response to stimuli often before the stimuli even have reached our conscious awareness. This is why we can literally jump back when we catch a glimpse of a snake on the trail ahead of us, only to later find out that it was just a stick. If it had been a snake, our unconscious jumping back could have actually saved our life. Jumping back when it turns out to be a stick might be embarrassing, but it's not life threatening. Get the idea? Emotional regulation is the sweet spot in our experience where we are able to feel the emotion and think about what it means at the same time. This ability to think and feel simultaneously allow us the opportunity to initiate, inhibit, or modulate action—all with conscious awareness.

Young children can't do this yet. Remember, emotions develop well before thoughts, language, or self-control. The neocortex is the last part of the brain to become fully functional. During their first years of life, young children have no way of understanding or regulating the flood of emotions and sensations they experience. Again, those emotions are our first survival strategy, moving us toward what is needed and away from what is dangerous. The problem is that infants have no ability to physically move toward or away; nor can they intentionally initiate or inhibit their reactions. They are completely at the mercy of their caregiver. In other words, they aren't choosing their response, or trying to manipulate the parent as is sometimes believed.

I still remember when my visiting aunt chastised me for going upstairs to pick up my crying infant daughter. "You are spoiling her! I never did that with my kids." My response? I smiled as I picked up my daughter and said, "Well it's a good thing she's not your daughter" (suffice it to say she was never my favorite aunt). I knew my daughter was only expressing a need. My attuned response was helping her to learn that she is seen, she matters, and she is safe.

Attuned parents recognize and accept their role in helping children hear and interpret the messages emotions deliver. They don't ignore emotions or shame the child for having them. In this way, attuned parents are the child's primary teachers of emotional regulation. Emotional regulation simply means that we learn how to adaptively respond to the range of emotions we experience.

It is through these attuned interactions that children learn what message the emotion is delivering and what appropriate action (or inaction) should ensue. In essence, emotional regulation is really a form of arousal regulation. How do I "hear" the message of emotion and use it to move me toward survival and growth? The ability to experience the emotion (limbic brain) and to think about the emotion (prefrontal cortex) refers to our window of tolerance.

This concept, coined by Dan Siegel, noted physician and researcher on interpersonal neurobiology, refers to the space within which our thinking mind and feeling mind are working together.[9] There is a "sweet spot" in which we can notice the stimuli coming at us, think about it rationally, and choose a response that is most adaptive in the moment. When we are outside this window of tolerance, our thinking brain gets highjacked by our nervous system such that we are only feeling, (i.e., hyperarousal), or numbing (i.e., hypo-arousal, neither thinking nor feeling). In these moments, our nervous system moves into the heightened arousal of survival mode. People vary in how wide or narrow their window of tolerance is. Some are able to feel their emotions and choose their response. Others are much more reactive to their emotions. Not surprisingly, this window gets formed early via our interactions with others. Luckily, it is changeable.

Attuned interaction between parent and child is necessary for optimal development. Unfortunately, attuned parenting isn't every child's experience. For attunement to happen, parents need to have a certain level of self-awareness. They need to have learned how to regulate their own emotions so the crying or temper tantrum of their two-year old doesn't throw them into a tailspin. They have to be secure enough in who they are that they can freely pay attention to another without becoming overwhelmed. This can be difficult if they are locked in their own internal prison.

The good news is that attunement doesn't have to be perfect for kids to have healthy development. In fact, some research suggest attunement only has to be at 30% to be developmentally helpful.[10] Google "Still Face Experiment" to watch this demonstrated between a mother and her child. In the moments of missed attunement, in which we were not available to soothe the child or we didn't realize she was upset, it's all about how we repair the connection. How we take responsibility for missing her cue and fixing it. We let her know we are here now. We help her make sense of what happened so she can see that it is over and that she is safe.

It's through such repair the child learns that broken connections can be restored. They trust that it can happen. We are resilient creatures but if the repair doesn't happen, we are left to make sense of this bad experience on our own. Like my concluding at age five that fighting leads to abandonment, we can get stuck in survival mode, bathed in a stress response that keeps us protected (and alive) but not able to grow. The foundation of our internal prison is poured.

Lots of pressure on the parent, huh? Indeed. In fairness, I believe that, with few exceptions, parents are doing the very best they can, given their own experiences. I frequently remind my clients of this. When exploring my clients' childhood experiences, it is in service of understanding the early programming that was installed. We're trying to understand the pattern—not vilify the parent (or others who were influential during the childhood years).

Henry Wadsworth Longfellow wrote: "If we could read the secret history of our enemies, we should find in each man's life sorrow and suffering enough to disarm all hostility."[11] This sums it up. Sometimes our parents weren't the recipients of attuned parenting themselves. Sometimes they are fighting their own depression or anxiety. Sometimes they are working so hard to provide for their families that they have very little time to actually be with them. It's complicated. We have to remember that parents aren't immune to incarceration either.

As you can probably surmise from the introduction, mine was not an experience of attuned parenting. My mother was depressed, and my father was anxious. It was hard for them to regulate their own emotions, so how could they have possibly been attuned to mine? Any uncomfortable emotion I experienced (e.g., anger, sadness, loneliness) was a messenger of not feeling connected. Rather than being interpreted as a plea for connection, however, my emotions were ignored, or worse, met with a heavy sigh, an eyeroll, and a passing comment about my being "too much."

Looking back, I realize my parents shut my emotions down because they didn't know what to do with them, not because there was something inherently wrong with me. In fairness, I now realize they were just doing with me what their parents did with them. In true midwestern fashion, we didn't address emotions, we ignored them.

I recall one incident in which I got really angry because I thought the babysitter was favoring my brother by letting him stay up while I had to go to bed. In fairness, now I know that the situation was more a function of his ADD than her permissiveness, but I didn't know it then. When I raised the issue with the sitter, she told me that wasn't what was happening and to mind my own business. In short, my concerns were dismissed. I remember stomping to my room and slamming the door. Still seething, I picked up my baton and smashed it into my bedroom door (it was the 1970s, don't judge the baton thing). The force of the blow put a hole in the door. Despite the loud thud, nobody came to check on me. In fact, the whole incident was ignored. I returned from school the next day and the hole was filled with wood filler. Again, no comment. It was like it never happened. My experience wasn't one of attuned connection and understanding; it was one of invisibility and shutdown.

In my family, we were trained not to name the elephant in the room. When I dared to name it, I was told I was mistaken. My experience and perceptions were of no interest. Because I, like every other developing child, was wired to stay connected, I learned to trade my own perceptions for what was more palatable to those around me. Construction of my internal prison continued.

# ♟ EMOTIONAL REGULATION

Check out this list of primary emotions:

| | | |
|---|---|---|
| Fear | Joy | Pain |
| Anger | Surprise | Interest |
| Sad | Disgust/Shame | Excitement |

How did these emotions get expressed or shut down
in your family during your early childhood years?

_____

_____

_____

_____

_____

_____

What does it look like now when you experience
these emotions?

_____

_____

_____

_____

_____

_____

_____

_____

## ATTACHMENT

The way caregivers respond to and interact with the child wires the way the child learns to interact in relationships. Drs. John Bowlby and Mary Ainsworth were among the earliest proponents of the idea that the nature of the connection between infant and caregiver (i.e., the attunement) sets the stage for the child's emotional development and sense of security.[12] In a nutshell, attachment theory suggests that when primary caregivers are attuned—sensitive and responsive to the child's needs—the child develops a sense of security, which simply means they believe they belong and are protected. They matter. They are understood. They are seen. This sense of security is precisely what makes it possible for them then to go out and explore the world. They know they have a safe place to land if they run into trouble.

Indeed, studies of attachment actually focus on what happens when the child is separated from a parent or experiences stress or fear. In these moments, the attachment system dictates how the child regulates his emotions. When frightened or upset, a securely attached child seeks physical closeness with the caregiver and allows himself to be soothed upon reunion (i.e., emotionally regulated). An insecurely attached child does not. For the insecurely attached child, the caregiver is not a source of safety and soothing so the child is left to learn how to regulate emotions on his own.

Four distinct patterns of attachment, or what I like to call adaptive strategies, have been established.[13]

**Secure attachment** is evidenced in children who become upset when they are separated from their caregiver but are easily soothed upon being reunited. Securely attached children seek out caregivers for reassurance and comfort when they are scared and the caregiver is able to help them regulate their emotions.

An **insecure attachment** pattern can show up in three ways:

- **Avoidant attachment** is evidenced when children avoid caregivers—not preferring them to strangers when seeking emotional support. This type of attachment can be the result of a mis-attuned parent/caregiver, one who fails to read the child's signals or simply misinterprets them. Avoidantly attached children learn that not only will they not receive comfort from the caregiver, but that they might actually receive punishment or be shamed for seeking it out.

- In **ambivalent attachment**, children are upset when the parent is unavailable. They actively seek them out. However, when the parent does return, the ambivalently attached child rejects their attempts to provide comfort.

- Finally, **disorganized attachment** is revealed in children who show a mix of behaviors, sometimes seeking the parent and sometimes actively avoiding them. This is usually the result of inconsistent or unpredictable caregiving where the parent can sometimes be the source of comfort and other times the source of fear.

In sum, these early experiences form the blueprint for how the child views the world and her place within it. It's important to recognize that children can experience different attachment styles with different caregivers (based on experience). For example, you might have had a secure attachment with your mother who was well attuned, but an avoidant one with your father who was unpredictable.

As you may have guessed, these styles translate into adult attachment when the issue of security moves from caregiver to romantic partner. As adults, these attachment patterns are based on comfort with emotional closeness (e.g., depending on and being dependable for one's partner), and the degree of anxiety about being abandoned or rejected. I often ask clients to think about the first person they have the impulse to call when they are anxious or scared. Their answer usually reveals their person. If you didn't receive secure attachment, don't worry. You aren't doomed to a life sentence in prison. It's changeable. In the therapy world, this move from an insecure attachment style to a secure attachment style is called earned security. This move can happen when an insecurely attached person teams up with a securely attached person. It can also happen through therapy.

Clearly, emotional connection is every bit as important for development as are food and shelter. Maureen and Steve came to see me several years ago to work through the pain and grief of their third miscarriage. They decided to pursue overseas adoption. A few months later, they called me with the exciting news that they had just returned with little Sophia. However, the three-year-old child from the Ukrainian orphanage was tiny, much smaller than her age would suggest. She wouldn't speak. She wouldn't make eye contact. Maureen and Steve were worried. They couldn't connect. They were heartbroken but determined so they sought answers. A savvy physician specializing in international adoption provided them. She told the parents that a condition called "psychosocial short stature IPSS" also known as stress dwarfism or Kaspar Hauser syndrome was to blame. It's a condition caused by extreme emotional deprivation or stress.

In such case, the body actually stops secreting the growth hormone essential for normal physical and emotional development. It's as if the body knows it isn't safe to thrive where it is, so it hits the pause button, goes dormant and waits for spring. Luckily for Sophia, spring came when Steve and Maureen learned how to help her. They focused on honing their attunement to her. It took some time, but eventually their consistent warmth, affection, and responsiveness, along with loads of tender physical touch, reawakened her system. She began to thrive under their loving care. She left the solitary confinement her body imposed. She grew. She spoke. She connected.

This idea of needing more than just physical nutrition was brilliantly highlighted in the work of Dr. Harry Harlow in his study of rhesus monkeys.[14] Harlow, an American psychologist, was interested in the role of contact comfort (i.e., touch) in primate development. To explore this topic, Harlow put rhesus monkeys separated at birth from their actual monkey mothers in a cage with two surrogate "mothers." The first mother figure was covered in soft terry cloth but had no milk bottle. The second had a milk bottle but was made of wire. Harlow observed that the monkeys went to the wire mother long enough to drink the milk, but then spent the majority of their time snuggled with the terry cloth mother. Harlow's work produced early evidence about the importance of maternal touch in infant development.

John Bolwby also demonstrated the importance of emotional connection in his study of Eastern European children orphaned during World War II. These children were housed in institutional orphanages with adequate food, shelter, and healthcare; however, many of them did not develop normally, either physically or emotionally. Bowlby believed they were "touch starved."[15] "Failure to thrive" is a diagnosis attributed to children who aren't in line with weight standards for their age. While this is commonly related to poor nutrition, emotional neglect or abuse can also be to blame.

More recent research connects our childhood experiences to adult outcomes. The Adverse Childhood Experiences (ACE) Study is one of the most comprehensive studies on the relationship between childhood experiences and adult health. This study, a joint effort between the Centers for Disease Control and Kaiser Permanente, started in 1995 and  followed thousands of participants from childhood into adulthood. Adverse childhood experiences were grouped into three categories: abuse (e.g., physical, sexual, emotional), neglect (e.g., emotional and physical), and household challenges (e.g., parental mental illness, family violence, substance abuse, or incarcerated relative).

Findings reveal a clear connection between these childhood stressors and later health and social problems, including pulmonary, heart, and liver disease, depression, illicit drug use, intimate partner violence, mental health issues and suicide attempts.[16] Of course, this connection is correlational, not causal. In other words, having adverse childhood experiences isn't an automatic life sentence. It just means that in the absence of attunement, poor outcomes are more likely.

Now that you have a basic idea of the foundational concepts of attunement, brain development, attachment, emotional regulation, and childhood stressors, you can begin to understand how our view of self and our place in the world are formed. When we have the benefit of attunement and secure attachment, we thrive. We are open to adventure secure in the knowledge that we belong. When we don't have it, we learn to lock parts of ourselves away. We prioritize survival rather than growth. Let's see how this played out for one of my clients.

Sixty-year-old Mary recounted the painful memories of her adolescence. At age sixteen, she found herself alone with a military doctor. Her mother was in the waiting room. Mary hadn't started her menstrual cycle. By most accounts she was late. The doctor could not explain the delay. His decided lack of bedside manners left Mary thinking there was something wrong with her. He didn't try to reassure her. She concluded she was defective. As we talked about the context of this experience, it became clear that Mary's body had gone into a sort of survival mode. It stopped developing. Why would it do that? For the answer, we need to look beyond Mary's body. We need to look at what was happening around her. We need to understand her experience of disconnect.

To the outsider, everything about Mary's life looked normal. Her father was a highly respected military officer. As officer's kids, Mary and her siblings were on constant display in the community. They were reminded that they were a reflection of their father. They were to lead by example. They needed to be perfect. There was no room for any missteps that could negatively impact their father's military career. The children did their part to perpetuate the happy family story. But it wasn't always so happy.

A different version of her father lived behind the walls of their home. Mary's father served three consecutive tours of duty in Vietnam. His tours began when she was nine years old. He returned home for good when she was eleven. At that point, Mary noticed that he was a very different father than he had been three years earlier. Before, he was a happy jokester and a doting father and husband. He was patient and kind. Upon return, his jokes were replaced with irritable complaints. Instead of doting, he exploded in anger, or withdrew to the basement.

He started drinking heavily, and her parents starting fighting. Mary said she and her sister huddled together at the top of the stairs, silent witnesses to the chaos downstairs. Mary was scared and confused. "Who was this man?" she thought. She dared to ask what was wrong. "Nothing is wrong," her mother said. "Don't ask questions," her father snapped. She knew there was a problem but was told she was wrong. She stopped trusting her own perception.

Mary tried to believe them and play along. After all, they were the adults and she was supposed to be able to trust them. She tried to accommodate by staying quiet. She stopped asking questions. She stopped listening to her gut. She learned to distract and pretend. She spent more time at school. She laughed louder with her friends. She was building the walls of her prison while keeping up appearances as expected. But her body knew the truth. Her body registered the stress. It stopped growing. It moved into survival mode. Mary's body confirmed the truth her mind was trying to deny.

In truth, home wasn't safe. Mary was living in a field of emotional landmines, never certain when one would explode. It turns out that her father was suffering from Post-Traumatic Stress Disorder (PTSD), something that wasn't widely addressed back in the 1970s. As an officer, he felt it wasn't okay to ask for help. He turned to alcohol to quiet the demons that haunted him. He withdrew or he exploded. What else could he do? Mary's assessment was right all along. Her body hit pause. Survival first.

Eventually her father entered a treatment program and got the help he needed. The family recovered. With family therapy and time, relationships were repaired. Mary's period came.

Mary's story provides a wonderful example of how attachment can change over time. With respect to her father, Mary started with secure attachment. She moved to insecure attachment when her father became unpredictable with his alcohol use. He was no longer safe. She returned to securely attached after he successfully completed treatment and the family was able to make sense of the whole experience.

In summary, experiences with our primary caretakers early in life shape the way we learn to show up in the world. Because our brains are still under construction, we must rely on those around us to help us make sense of the world. Known as "internal working models," these become our template of how we view ourselves, others, and the world around us. If we are attuned and responded to appropriately, we feel secure. We know that we can count on someone to have our back. The world seems predictable. We learn that we have agency. We believe that we are seen and that we matter. We grow. When children feel secure, they actually become more independent, more adventurous, not less. It's fear or insecurity that shuts us down. It keeps us small and imprisoned.

This security doesn't give us immunity from unfamiliar, scary, or traumatic events. Bad things inevitably happen. Security helps us move through those experiences in an adaptive way because we have people who can help us make sense of what happened. They can regulate their own emotions enough to be available to attune to us and our distress. They assure us that we are loved and connected in spite of this bad thing. They assure us that this bad thing is just a bad thing, not a reflection of our basic worth.

In this context, we learn to tolerate the stresses of life and to become stronger because of them. In the absence of this secure connection, we are much more likely to get stuck. Fear shuts us down. Remember, as children, we aren't equipped to make sense of the bad things on our own. We're egocentric in our explanation. Without guidance, we often end up blaming ourselves. We start to believe there is something wrong with us. Trauma ensues. The body remembers. We get trapped in the prison of our own making.

**EXTRA CREDIT**

## ★ YOUR ATTACHMENT STYLE

To get a sense of your current attachment style, read the descriptions below. This quiz comes from the brilliant work of Dr. Diane Poole Heller.[17] Read the questions, thinking of one person at a time. Remember, you can have different attachment styles to different people.

### Secure

Do you easily and clearly ask to have your own needs met?

Are you affectionate with those with whom you feel close?

Do you leave when things are too off in a relationship, knowing there are other great options for fulfilling relationships?

Do you want to be close to others, find it easy to connect, and expect relationships to go well?

### Avoidant

Does closeness cause you to create distance afterwards?

Do you struggle to maintain eye contact?

Do you often judge others for not being more self-sufficient?

Do you find emotional, effusive, or dramatic people annoying?

How important is your career and work in comparison to your personal relationships?

Do you have trouble knowing or asking for what you need?

### Ambivalent (Anxious)

Do you often find yourself yearning for people who are unavailable to you?

Do you sometimes apologize for things you haven't done simply because you fear upsetting or losing the other person? _____

Does your partner sometimes describe you as clingy or needy? _____

Do you feel like you typically give more than you receive in relationships? If so, do you often end up feeling resentful toward the other person, even to the point of holding a grudge? _____

When you are alone, do you regularly feel abandoned, stressed, hurt, or angry? _____

Do you find yourself complaining a lot and overlooking or dismissing caring behaviors of others? _____

## Disorganized (Fearful Avoidant)

Do you often struggle with mixed messages from other people (come here, go away)? _____

Do you sometimes experience an inexplicable fear when you reach a certain level of intimacy with others?

_____

Do you often disconnect, dissociate, or become confused in relationships? _____

Do you experience unpredictable sudden shifts of states (for example, switching from joy and happiness to fear and anger?)

_____

Have you ever experienced deep longings to connect with others and then inexplicably want to get away from them?

_____

Pay attention to your dominant style. These questions begin to help you see the adaptive strategies you took on in an effort to manage connection in your life, and thus survival. It can inform if and how you become imprisoned later, as well as clues to your escape.

## CHAPTER 2

# GETTING STUCK

Cheryl made her way slowly from the waiting room to my office. She dropped her coat on the floor and plopped down in the chair. I waited for her to speak. She avoided my eyes as she said, "I can't believe I did it again. You must think I'm an idiot." As we talked, Cheryl admitted she was back in contact with an old flame she had been trying hard to forget. The relationship had been toxic for her. "I'm so ashamed," she said. "Why do I keep going back to him? A part of me knew I should ignore his text, but another part replied before I could stop myself. I'm so stupid! I actually convinced myself it would be different this time."

"How did it go?" I asked halfheartedly, already knowing the answer. With a sigh, she replied, "It was the same as always. He only texted me because he was lonely, and sucker that I am, I of course told him to come over. We hung out most of the night and agreed to meet for lunch the next day. He never showed up. All my messages went to straight to voicemail. He ghosted me again. I am so humiliated! Why am I so stuck?"

Cheryl's experience is far from unique. A part of her was so desperate for connection, it overrode another part of her that knew it was futile with this man. Like Cheryl, we all have a variety of aspects, personalities, voices, ego states, or parts (pick what you want to call them) in our internal world. Believe it or not, this multiplicity of mind is actually normal. We can observe our parts if we pay attention. For example, when my alarm goes off early in the morning, one part of me says "Rise and shine, let's go for a run!" Fairly quickly another part chimes in, "Noooooooo. This bed is so warm. Let's just hit snooze. You deserve a break." And the internal conversation begins. A similar thing happens when there is chocolate ice cream in the freezer. "Eat the ice cream" says one part. "Don't eat the ice cream" says another. You get the idea. Internal conversations are happening all the time.

All these parts are trying to help us, but they don't always have the same agenda. For example, the part that wants me to get up early and run wants me to be healthy. It knows I am more focused with my clients after I have moved my body. The part that wants me to stay in bed is also trying to help. It knows I work hard and wants me to be able to rest. Both are trying to help—they just have very different strategies. Much of the time, these parts function well together to help us find our place in the world. Sometimes, however, the parts stop working together and start fighting for control. Cheryl's story is a good example of this. Like many of us, she found herself repeating a cycle she knew was damaging.

Why do we get caught in such negative cycles? As you can probably guess, our patterns are adaptations to our early relational interactions. For better or for worse, these experiences form the initial template for how we show up in the world. How does this work, you ask? To answer this question, we begin with the role of learning, memory, and pattern matching.

## LEARNING AND MEMORY

From a brain perspective, "learning" simply refers to neurons wiring together. "What fires together wires together" is the accepted phrase in neuroscience circles.[1] The wiring or firing together forms a patterned response, one that becomes an automatic response that can occur outside of conscious awareness. Memories are actually stored "learnings" based on experience. There are two main categories of memories: explicit and implicit. Explicit memories are typically what we think about when it comes to memory. Explicit memories are formed with conscious awareness. They are fact based, semantic descriptions. Given this, explicit memories aren't formed until around ages three or four, the age when our prefrontal cortex is coming online and we have gained command of language. The description of your childhood bedroom, or your fine dining experience last weekend both come from your explicit memory. Explicit memories are recalled on demand like stories.

Unlike explicit memories, implicit memories occur outside of our conscious awareness. Thus, this type of memory is forming from the moment we are born (some suggest even while in utero). Implicit memories are connected to emotions, sensations, and behaviors but not to narrative stories. Whether explicit or implicit, our brain uses the memory of previous experience to inform what is happening in the present. It's trying to help us discern the most adaptive response. When it comes to our own incarceration, a particular type of implicit memory, known as procedural memory, is of particular interest.

Here's an example of procedural memory. Remember the first time you got behind the wheel of car? The nervousness or excitement you may have felt? The sweatiness of your palms? The vigilance you employed? Adjusting the mirrors just so? Making sure your hands were firmly planted at 10 and 2 o'clock? How careful you were? Full stops? Clumsily using your blinkers to signal turns and lane changes? Jerking the wheel as you changed lanes? Fast forward a few years and think about how you drive now. I am guessing if I were to ride with you today, I might find you driving down the road, eating a cheeseburger, talking on the phone, and still managing to arrive safely at your destination with no problem.

How did this happen? Procedural memory. Procedural memories are those that wired together for specific procedures (as opposed to incidences) and allow us to seamlessly function without the need for our full attention. It's a brilliant adaptation. I think about procedural memories as particular software programs that have been minimized on our internal desktop. You can't see them, and you aren't paying attention to them, but they are operating nonetheless. This is actually very helpful because, just like your laptop, if multiple programs are "open" at the same time, your attention can be scattered. It is messy. It can be confusing—too much to pay attention to.

Procedural memory shortcuts the actions you frequently use. It functions without sucking up all of your attention. This frees up our conscious mind (the desktop) to pay closer attention to what is right in front of us, scanning for current threats or safety. We aren't free to scan if we are busy trying to remember all the steps necessary for driving the car. When our attention is diverted, we are vulnerable. Procedural memory is the brain's way of optimizing performance. Most of the time this works seamlessly. We don't have think about how to walk, hold a fork, wash our hair, or ride a bike. We just do it. This is wonderfully efficient unless the program takes over and operates in conditions for which it wasn't meant. Why would this happen? To answer that question, we have to understand pattern matching.

## PATTERN MATCHING

Fireworks explode, and my client responds by diving under the table. Someone drops a heavy suitcase near another client in an airport and she drops to the floor with her hands over her head. Why this response? As Iraq/Afghanistan combat veterans, their tours of duty were over, but their brains were still on high alert. In the theater of war, diving for cover literally saved their lives. So diving for cover on the 4th of July and at the airport are examples of how procedural memory operates automatically. From a survival standpoint, it's better to be wrong than it is to be dead (remember the snake versus the stick example from the previous chapter?). How did this procedural memory get triggered? The brain was doing its best to "pattern match."

Pattern matching is another way our brain has adapted for survival. We were built to learn from every experience with the intention of becoming better at the game of survival. Every thought, sensation, feeling, and image triggers neuronal firing and synaptic connections. These repeating "firings" (i.e., experiences with the world) are the definition of learning. They become a pattern or a template that we use to interact with those around us. In other words, our experiences, either through repetition or trauma, get put into a memory file. This rich, multi-dimensional file contains all the aspects of the experience--words, sounds, smells, and tastes—all the senses. When working properly, it's seamless. The file for riding a bike gets pulled, and you do it again and again without falling off. Ditto for driving a car or catching a ball. It just happens with very little thinking.

For my clients, the procedural memory was set with the sound of mortar fire and its sulfurous smell. It was a traumatic experience, with high emotions and the possibility of death. When any of those sensory inputs were experienced later, the pattern triggered an automatic dive for cover. Like my stumbling on the steps, their bodies reacted before their minds caught up. Unlike my experience, however, their response wasn't contextually appropriate.

Still not sure what I mean by pattern matching? Read the following paragraph to experience it in action:

> I cnduo't bvleiee I I culod aulaclty uesdtannrd I
> I was rdnaieg. Unisg the icndeblire pweor of the
> 31ind31 31ind, aocdcrnig to rseecrah at Cmabrigde
> Uinervtisy, it dseno't mttaer in I oderr the lterets
> in a I are, the olny irpoamtnt 31ind31 is I the frsit
> and lsat ltteer be in the rhgit pclae. The rset can be a
> taotl mses and you can I raed it whoutit a pboerlm.
> I is bucseae the 31ind31 31ind deos not raed ervey
> ltteer by istlef, but the I as a wlohe. Aaznmig, huh?
> Yaeh and I awlyas tghhuot slelinpg was ipmorantt!
> See if I fdreins can raed I too.[2]

See what I mean? When something completely new or potentially confusing appears, your brain seizes on one aspect of it to try to pattern match—figure it out based on past experience. While this example was about how we read, the same idea applies to all our interactions. Our brain seizes on certain aspects of the situation (in this case, the first and last letter), ignoring others (what was in the middle), and goes to work matching those aspects to prior experiences (words). In other examples, the match may come from the smell, the sound, or the way something or someone looks. The brain is so intent on trying to make "sense" of what it perceives, and thus evaluate safety, that it will force a match even if it isn't perfect. I think of it like the voice or facial recognition software on detective shows—the file sorts through all the possible matches at lightning speed then lands on a match. In search of safety, the match may be well less than 100%, but no matter. Again, it's better to be wrong than to be dead.

Pattern matching is absolutely necessary for our functioning. It is wonderful when it works and torturous when it is wrong. My client Steve's brain seized on his wife's tone of voice, ignoring her actual words and the concerned expression on her face. Her tone matched that of his father's when he was trying to humiliate Steve. In those moments, the meaning Steve construed was "I am under attack," rather than "my wife wants to understand me." The result? He fought back. Professionally, my client Sabrina focused on the one critical comment she received after a workshop she presented, ignoring all the positive feedback. The criticism "matched" what she felt as a child when she felt stupid. The result? She turned down a lucrative opportunity to present her work at another conference.

The collateral damage is that no new learning can take place when the body is in that survival mode. Remember Mary? We can't be in survival and growth mode simultaneously. In other words, no new adaptive information can be added to our warehouse of memory files when we are in survival mode. Why does this matter? Because in survival mode, we go on automatic pilot, which sets us up to use strategies that aren't actually helpful. Without conscious awareness, it never occurs to us to question the strategy. As Einstein stated: Doing the same thing over and over again and expecting different results is the definition of insanity.

## BUILDING BEGINS

What keeps us stuck, what forms the bars of the cells that keep us fragmented, separated from the best parts of us, are the negative beliefs we take on about ourselves. Sometimes these beliefs come directly from what we were told by adults. Other times they are based on the conclusions we made based on those interactions. As you learned in the last chapter, when our interactions with caregivers are attuned, we feel secure and safe in the connection. We can count on them to help us make sense of what is happening to us. This connection is especially important when it comes to emotionally overwhelming experiences, like trauma.

In emotionally overwhelming experiences, children usually are unable to make accurate sense of what is happening. Attuned adults can help the child to see that while a bad thing did happen (the house caught on fire, the car wrecked, dad went away), it is over. They can help the child trace the beginning, the middle, and the end. The attuned adult can reassure the child that she is not alone and that she is safe now. Bad thing over. Through this attunement, we develop positive beliefs about ourselves, others, and the world: I am enough. I am loveable. I matter. I did my best. I have choice. I am strong. Others are trustworthy. Others help. The world is good.

When this attuned sense-making exercise between adult and child doesn't happen, the child is left to figure it out on his own.

Developmentally, children tend to blame themselves for whatever bad thing that has happened. The house must have caught on fire because I am evil. Dad must have left because I was bad. My mother wouldn't drink if I wasn't such a burden. We weave together an explanatory story that we tell ourselves so many times we start to believe it. It becomes wired into memory via its repetition. Over time, it becomes the default lens through which we interpret the world. We forget that our belief is based on a story we made up. It's just a story, but we take it as truth. When the beliefs are negative, we learn to shut down the more spontaneous, playful, curious parts of ourselves. We trade our joy for an orange jumpsuit. I have heard many different iterations of such beliefs from my clients. I have recognized them in myself as well. They tend to include one or more of the following themes.[3]

## INADEQUACY

The first is some version of inadequacy or "there is something wrong with me." We make ourselves responsible for our incarceration. We whisper phrases to ourselves like "I am not lovable," "I am stupid," "I am defective," "I'm too much," or "I am inadequate." My client Clyde came to see me after a nasty divorce. He was convinced he was unlovable.

As we explored this belief, Clyde recounted an early memory (around age four) in which he was stuck in the "time out" chair, yet again. He said he remembers crying as he sat there thinking, "Mommy is mad at me again." It was a short jump from that thought to "I can never get it right," and then to his conclusion of "I am unlovable." The pattern was set. Whenever someone was mad at him, it confirmed his belief of being unlovable. Through our work, Clyde realized his mother was actually depressed and very unhappy during those years (his parents later divorced). At age four, however, Clyde only knew she always seemed to be angry at him. Her inability to attune to his emotional state left him to make sense of it with naivete of a four year old: I am unlovable.

## RESPONSIBILITY

The second theme centers around responsibility. We make ourselves responsible for our incarceration. We say things like "I did it wrong," "it's all my fault," or "I should have known better." My client, Martha, came to see me after a failed relationship. She said she can't stop thinking about what she did wrong. Thoughts of "what if" kept her up at night. "Maybe if I would have given more, maybe if I weren't so needy, maybe if I would have made more money…"

As we explored belief, it became clear that Martha learned this strategy of blaming herself early in childhood. She said her dad was only interested in talking to her about what she could do or how she performed. He was talkative and complementary when she brought home straight A's on her report card. He gave her the silent treatment when she lost the election for student body president. It never occurred to Martha that her father's affection should have been unconditional. She only knew that to stay connected to her father she had to win.

## CHOICE/CONTROL

"I have no choice or control" forms a third theme of negative beliefs. We believe that we are powerless and weak. "I can't handle it," we think. "I cannot succeed." "I will never get what I need." Our experiences in the world seem to confirm this idea. When we call, nobody comes. We become victims, defenseless against the stronger adults around us. We start to believe we can't possibility succeed. We stop trying. "What is the point?" we think. Learned helplessness ensues.

At 28, my client Brenda came to see me because of debilitating anxiety. She agonized over every decision, doubting herself and changing her mind repeatedly. As we talked about her history, Brenda said that as a child and all through high school, her mother made every decision for her--from what to wear, what classes to take, and what activities to join. Brenda's protests were met with "mother knows best." Never having choices led Brenda to the conclusion that she couldn't possibly be trusted to have control of her own life. She stopped trying.

## SAFETY/VULNERABILITY

The fourth theme centers around safety and vulnerability. "I can't trust anyone" we think. "The world isn't safe," we conclude. "I can't protect myself," we say. "Everyone is out to get me." We see danger everywhere and fear sets in. We feel unsafe, even with those we love. Doug and Jackie came to see me about their marriage. According to Doug, Jackie's depression and tendency to always assume the worst was ruining their relationship. As we explored Jackie's pattern, she told me the story of the elaborate ruse her family enacted to shield her from the reality of her father's terminal cancer. She was only six years old. She said she remembers taking lots of family vacations. She thought they were rich to be able to travel so much!

Only later did she find out their "vacations" were actually trips to treatment centers for her father. Their bank account was near empty. She believed her mother when she told her that her father was losing weight because he was dieting and his hair was falling out because he was old. Nobody mentioned chemotherapy. She thought she was lucky to have him around so much. She didn't realize he was out of a job. She bitterly said, "I didn't even get to say goodbye because I didn't know he was dying." She said she felt stupid for not knowing—embarrassed that everyone was in on the "secret" of her father's illness but her.

Of course she concluded that the world isn't a safe place. She couldn't trust the people who were supposed to love her the most to tell her the truth and to help her make sense of a terrible loss. Better to keep her guard up.

From a developmental standpoint, the beliefs we hold about ourselves, others, and the world become powerful predictors of our functioning. This happens even if the beliefs we hold are outside of our conscious awareness. For example, notice the subtle changes in your body as you read each of the following statements:

I am lovable.

I am defective.

I am powerful.

I am powerless.

The world is safe.

The world is scary.

Our beliefs set the stage for how we show up in the world by literally changing how we feel in our body. The belief informs the meaning we make and thus how our nervous system responds. Remember my softball and acorn experience? As you have learned, this interaction between belief and physiology literally changes how we experience the world. Are we in defensive shut down mode or are we open for connection and growth? When asked what the most important question in the world was, Einstein reportedly responded, "Is the universe friendly?" He was onto something. The way you answer this question informs the way you approach the world.

**YOUR TURN**

## ♟ NEGATIVE BELIEFS

Review the four categories of negative beliefs.

### Inadequacy

There is something wrong with me. I am unlovable. I am worthless. I am too much.

### Responsibility

I did it wrong. It's all my fault. I should have known better.

### Choice/Control

I can't handle it. I can't succeed. I have no control.

### Safety/Vulnerability

I can't trust anyone. I can't protect myself. The world isn't safe.

**Which ones resonate with you?**

_____

_____

_____

_____

_____

_____

_____

_____

_____

_____

Review the attachment styles from Chapter 1:

## Secure

I am confident that people will be there for me. I can ask for what I need. I expect relationships to go well. I can leave if they aren't.

## Anxious/Ambivalent

I worry that my partner will leave me. I can be clingy and needy. When I'm alone I feel abandoned. I feel like I give more than I get in relationships.

## Avoidant

I avoid emotions and their drama. I am annoyed with those who aren't self-sufficient. I don't know or ask for what I need. After closeness in relationships, I create distance.

## Disorganized

I long to be close to others then push them away when it happens. My emotional state can shift rapidly. I get confused and disoriented in close relationships.

What connection do you see between your attachment style and your pattern of negative beliefs?

_____

_____

_____

_____

_____

_____

_____

## THE MAKING OF A PRISONER

When we are riddled with negative beliefs, shame sets in. Shame is broadly defined as "a painful feeling of humiliation or distress caused by the consciousness of wrong or foolish behavior" (Merriam-Webster). Shame says, "I am bad" while guilt says, "I did something bad." Shame and guilt are both emotions born out of social interactions. They are powerful behavioral motivators. When we feel guilt, we are motivated to change our behavior in an effort to belong; however, when we feel shame, we assume we are unworthy and hide from connection. From an evolutionary survival perspective, not belonging is a sure recipe for death. I've got little chance of survival in the wilderness alone. We learn to hide the aspects of ourselves we believe are shameful--the parts that hold all the negative beliefs described earlier: there is something wrong with me, it's my fault, I can't trust, the world isn't safe.

As the examples from Clyde, Martha, Brenda, and Jackie reveal, these parts of ourselves become prisoners locked away from any interactions with others. They become the scapegoats for the family system, unwittingly assuming the blame for their parents' inability to deal with their own dysfunctional patterns and pain. Sadly, we can have more than one prisoner. While they are typically formed around early childhood experiences, they can also be formed at other times in our life that are highly stressful or traumatic.

My client Carrie's story is illustrative. Carrie, a highly successful executive, came to me because, in her words, she sabotages all her romantic relationships. She described her father as the very successful coach of the town's baseball team. Her dad was a legend in the community. Her brother was equally a star as the winning pitcher in three consecutive state championships. Carrie's birthday happens to fall right in the middle of baseball season.

She smiled as she recalled the celebrations her mother would create—a fabulous cake, beautiful candles, and tons of gifts; however, her brother and father were never there. Carrie said she once overheard her mother imploring her dad to forgo baseball practice (not even an actual game) "just this once" so the whole family could be together to celebrate Carrie. He refused. Carrie concluded she wasn't good enough or she didn't matter enough for her dad to be there. She couldn't figure out what was wrong with her. She felt shame. She tried to outrun the shame by becoming wildly successful in a male-dominated field.

Despite the success, the belief of not being good enough was already woven deep into her implicit memory—a negative belief of which she had little conscious awareness. The result? Whenever a man was interested in her romantically, she rejected him before he rejected her. This was her way of taking control, sidestepping the shame of what she was sure would come when men inevitably rejected her, just as she thought her father had. She couldn't allow herself to believe that she was worthy of such male attention.

Through our work, Carrie realized her dad always loved her dearly. It turns out his absence at her birthdays had much more to do with his own insecurity about his identity as a coach than it was about his love for her as a father. This realization allowed Carrie to loosen her grip on her belief of herself as unworthy.

## MEET THE GUARDS

Our adaptive strategies, or "parts" of us, turn into Guards when the system believes there is something to hide—something that will get in the way of our connection with others. On the face of it, the Guards' strategies can look positively adaptive. Remember my perfectionistic tendencies? It's the motivation for the strategy that turns them into Guards. Their job is to keep our prisoners locked away, out of public view. They are motivated by fear of the prisoner's escape. It's important to note that the Guards didn't start out as Guards. They may have had their sights set on being creative, adventurous, and carefree. Guards are often forced into service in the name of system survival. They take one for the good of the team.

All of our Guards, regardless of how kind or mean they appear, are trying to help us win the game of survival by managing our connections with others. This can mean being seen when it's safe (moving toward connection) or fighting or becoming invisible when it's not (moving away from connection).

How do the Guards learn their roles? Usually Guards have learned their strategies from watching and/or interacting with the influential people in our lives, like parents, other family members, teachers, or coaches. Our role models for better or worse. For example, I learned to be pleasing by watching my mother. She attempted to anticipate my father's every need and meet it before he could even ask. I learned caution by watching my father. He usually listed all the things that could go wrong in a situation or new adventure. Although he often came around, his first answer was usually "no."

Incarceration can also come from misplaced loyalty to our families. We start to believe that their fate is our fate. Conversations with my clients in this regard are revealing.

"My father wasn't successful so who am I to believe I could be? That's just who we are."

"My mother drinks and is depressed. So was her mother. That's why I can never be happy either."

"My mother was sick, always in bed. So was my aunt. I must have a poor constitution too. I shouldn't expect to feel good."

If we dare to consider life beyond our cell block, to have the thought that we might be different, we often receive swift reprimand. "Who do you think you are?" we hear. "What makes you so special?" they ask. Or, "you will never survive out there—we are just trying to protect you." We are given the message (again, implicitly or explicitly) that this state of affairs is just reality.

Often, we learn to treat the offending parts of ourselves the same way they were treated by our parents or other important adults in our lives. In my family, for example, the consistent denial of my needs led me to start denying my own. This was how my internal Critic learned his schtick. Mimicking my father, the Critic would tell me my needs were silly. I shouldn't even have any needs. It functioned to shut me down internally before my father had a chance to externally. In other words, the Critic helped me avoid the shame of rejection.

Because of their mandate, our Guards are convinced that we should resign ourselves to this particular cell block. If we want to fit in, we must embrace prison life as reality. In so doing, we have to let go of the idea that our lives could somehow be different than how they have always been--that we could somehow beat the history of depression, sadness, abuse, anxiety, addiction, underachievement, or other issues that have plagued the rest of our family.

We have to let go of the idea that we could never lose the chip that was placed squarely on our shoulder by our father, and his father before him, and his father before him, for generations before. It's a kind of intergenerational trauma, a legacy of burdened beliefs. For example, my father's anxiety didn't start with him; it came from his father (my grandfather). My grandfather's anxiety was passed down from his father (my great grandfather), a German immigrant trying to make a better life in America. See how it works?

Instead of letting go, we resign ourselves to this confinement because, despite being uncomfortable and stifling, it is familiar. The Guards know how to do this gig. We convince ourselves that it is better to be loyal to the dysfunction of what is than to risk going it alone into the unknown.

So who are the Guards? Let me introduce you. You may recognize them or others as part of your own internal world. Prisoners are protected by two types of Guards: the Managers and the Firefighters. They are described below. You may find your Guards hold varying degrees of masculine, feminine, or neutral energy.

## MANAGER GUARDS

Managers are proactive Guards. As their name implies, they are trying to manage the internal and external worlds so the prisoners don't get activated, rebel, and attempt an escape. Experience dictates that this leads to more shame. Their motto is "never again." Guards on the management team believe that if they anticipate, prepare, and control everything enough, the prisoners will stay contained. This means the internal world will stay calm and we'll stay connected to the people around us. In short, the Managers are trying to achieve attachment by optimizing our desirability to others. Although not exhaustive, the Manager's team includes the Pleaser, the Perfectionist, the Worrywart, the Critic, and the Logician. Each uses a slightly different strategy to maintain control.

## THE PLEASER

The Pleaser tries to keep us connected to others by managing our relationships with the outside world. The Pleaser uses all its skills to placate others. It believes that if it is pleasing enough everything will be okay. The Pleaser looks pretty, plays nice, and is overaccommodating. The Pleaser works very hard to keep the emotional temperature at an even 72 degrees so everyone is comfortable all the time. It doesn't trust others' ability to tolerate or even regulate their own temperatures, so it is vigilant to their reactions.

The Pleaser believes that the only way to keep its internal system calm is by keeping the external system calm. It doesn't realize it's okay for it to be calm even if others are not. Its early experience was that it was unsafe when others weren't calm. It's never felt like it had the luxury of considering its own needs. The Pleaser hopes that if it just gives enough, others will do the same in return. When that doesn't happen, the Pleaser concludes it just hasn't been pleasing enough.

## THE PERFECTIONIST

The Perfectionist believes that if it just does it perfectly, it won't disappoint anyone or give them reason to criticize it. The Perfectionist has learned from past experience that it gets no grace when it falls short. No room for error. Although the Perfectionist is often exhausted, fear of disappointing others creates the anxiety that fuels its forward motion. The Perfectionist never asks for help because it is convinced that others would see it as inadequate. Early experiences confirmed this, and it vowed never to expose such vulnerability again. If the Perfectionist falls short, it doubles down on its efforts, working harder and harder. It doesn't occur to the Perfectionist that this is an impossible long-term strategy.

## THE WORRYWART

The Worrywart is constantly on the lookout for what could go wrong. For this reason, the Worrywart is rarely present in the moment. It's trying desperately to see five steps ahead, down the block, and around the corner. It believes if it can anticipate what could go wrong it can prevent it--or at least have a plan for dealing with it when it happens. It's the part Mark Twain famously references when he said: I've been through a lot of terrible things in my life, some of which have actually happened. The Worrywart often works nights. Unfortunately, as it dreams about what could go wrong in the future, it renders us unable to take in the good that is happening right now.

## THE CRITIC

The Critic patrols the walls of our internal world. It sees its job as that of quality control. To this end, it beats us up before those in the outside world get a chance to do it. The Critic reasons that if it does it first, we will course correct before others notice our shortcoming. While well intentioned, the Critic can become a bit of an overbearing drill sergeant, ripping us to shreds in an effort to motivate us. The Critic can also feel like a scolding judge, a scowling teacher, or an exasperated parent. The Critic is never satisfied. Sometimes its words are so harsh, we give up, retreating further into solitary confinement. It's hard to come back whole when you've been shredded so many times.

## THE LOGICIAN

The Logician only talks about things he deems rational and "true." It believes if it sticks to the facts, no one can disagree with it. The Logician has great disdain for any whiff of emotion. He has seen firsthand how quickly emotions get out of control, leading to chaos and pain. It vowed to never let this happen again. It's too dangerous. Too uncomfortable. The Logician is adamant that emotions are not to be trusted. It worships at the altar of rationality because it believes only rationality can sidestep conflict. The Logician wears a stoic face and appears quite rigid. Sadly, the Logician doesn't realize it can't selectively ignore emotions. It's an all or nothing proposition. The Logician doesn't know that while shutting down emotions protects it from pain, it also keeps it from joy.

## TAMMY'S STORY

Tammy came to see me because her marriage was in trouble. She said her husband of three years complained that he couldn't reach her. He was lonely and unhappy. He wanted her to get help before it was too late for their marriage. She told me she couldn't understand what she was doing wrong. We got to work.

Tammy was the middle child of three. Her parents divorced when she was young. She said she felt like there was very little time for her, and given that her parents were taking turns single-parenting three children, she was probably right. She described both of her parents as very strict. They had high standards that left no room for error.

She described herself as a mediocre student in school. Her dad wasn't happy about that, but he also didn't help her with her homework when she asked. He told her she should be able to figure it out on her own--like her siblings did. He said he didn't have time for her stupid questions, so she stopped asking. In her sophomore year, Tammy found a boyfriend who paid attention to her in ways that her parents didn't. He didn't care about her grades. He was warm. He laughed at her jokes and told her she was beautiful. He said he loved her. She got pregnant.

Tammy told me about the day she assembled both of her parents to tell them about the baby. She said she remembers sitting cross-legged on the living room floor in front of them. Her mother was nervous because she could tell that Tammy was about to say something big. Her dad shifted uncomfortably on the couch. "I'm pregnant," Tammy finally blurted out.

I asked her what she longed for the response to be in that moment. With tears in her eyes, she said "I wanted my dad to hug me and tell me everything would be alright. I wanted my mother to stroke my hair." She said she needed to know that they would love and accept her even if she had disappointed them. That she mattered more than her actions. That their love was truly unconditional. She didn't get that.

Instead, her mother started to cry, and her father refused to look at her. His only words were, "You will terminate this pregnancy." And he walked away. Stoney silence.

Her next memory is of him taking her to the clinic for an abortion. She saw protestors lining the walkways, condemning her for her "sin." She remembers her father checking her in at the front desk and the nurse asking whether Tammy wanted to have anesthesia. Before Tammy could respond, her father said, "No anesthesia. I want her to feel the pain of what she's done. Teach her a lesson." As though her shame wasn't big enough. As though she weren't already crushed by his disappointment. On the way home from the clinic her, father's only words were, "If you screw up again, you are out."

That's when the prison Guards got busy in Tammy's life. The Perfectionist showed up first. The Perfectionist pushed Tammy hard. The Critic came along too, constantly reminding her of her father's threat. She took it seriously. She'd seen him leave her mother. She knew he was capable of dismissing her as well. The Critic shut her down anytime she was tempted to ask for help. This Guard reminded her of when her father called her stupid for asking for help, so she didn't ask. Instead she pushed herself to work harder. She became a straight-A student. Her stomach ulcer was diagnosed the same week she was named valedictorian. She pushed through the pain.

Whenever she was tempted to slow down, the Critic stepped in and replayed the mental video of her father's look of disgust when she told him about the pregnancy. She heard his words "You'll be out." The Critic reminded her again and again that there was something inherently wrong with her. That she did something wrong. That she couldn't trust her own judgment. She ignored her body and pushed harder. Success came. She first graduated from college, then from graduate school. All with honors.

At her college graduation, her father told her he was proud of her. Tammy couldn't help but fear his pride in her was fleeting. One false move, the Critic reminded her, one more mistake and her father's disgust would return. She pushed on.

The Guards helped Tammy be successful. Unfortunately, they also kept her from being truly emotionally intimate with others. The Guards convinced her that hiding her vulnerability was the only way to avoid abandonment. Vulnerability was too risky—too needy, even with her husband. These Guards kept her from learning she could be loved and accepted, flaws and all. They kept her from realizing that the human condition is imperfect. I pointed this out to her, how the strategies—the Guards that made her "successful" and helped her to survive were also keeping her alone, not truly connected with others or even to her true self. She was dubious.

While she understood it in theory, she couldn't take it into her heart because that wasn't her lived experience. Her lived experience was that the ones who were supposed to love and protect her the most, made it conditional. How could she possibly allow herself to think it could be different? She concluded it was better not to risk it. Better to let her husband feel disconnected than to allow him to see her shame and leave her anyway.

---

**YOUR TURN**

**♟ NOTICE YOUR PROACTIVE MANAGER GUARDS**

Do you have a Pleaser, a Perfectionist, a Critic, a Worry Wort, a Logician, or other Manager Guards?

_____

_____

Under what conditions do they show up?

_____

_____

_____

---

## FIREFIGHTER GUARDS

The second type of Guards are called Firefighters. Unlike the proactive Managers, the Firefighter Guards are reactive. Firefighter Guards jump into action when the Manager Guards fail and the prisoner is loose. Their job is to get the prisoner back into its cell as soon as possible, again in an effort to mitigate shame. True to their name, Firefighters are singular in their focus of getting the prisoner contained (i.e., putting out the fire). Just like real firefighters, our internal Firefighter Guards don't care about how many windows are broken or how much water damage remains after they leave. The mess is just collateral damage. Their motto is "by any means necessary." This team includes the Warrior, the Distractor, and the Shut-Down-er. As with the Manager Guards, these examples are not meant to be exhaustive. Use them as a starting point to get to know your own.

## THE WARRIOR

The Warrior is a very active and powerful Guard. It's fiercely loyal to our protection. This is important to remember because our Warrior Guards often get a bad rap. When the Warrior smells a whiff of threat, it is on high alert, ready for a full-on fight. It uses anger and contempt to evoke fear in others. It feels justified in its fury and righteous in its attack. There is no remorse in sight. The Warrior can get big and scary, a tactic that instills fear. The Warrior pushes others into submission or just away. Ironically, its anger is often in direct proportion to the prisoners' pain. It much prefers the heat of anger than the pain of sadness. It vows never to allow itself to feel this pain. The Warrior revs up our sympathetic nervous system, often putting us into hyper-arousal, readying us for a fight and taking our prefrontal cortex (our thinking brain) out of commission.

## THE DISTRACTOR

The Distractor is master of changing the subject. As its name implies, it pulls our focus away from the shame of the prisoner. The Distractor worries that if we listen to the prisoners we will get trapped in their pain and sadness. No escape. The Distractor has learned to divert our attention in a variety of ways. These can include overworking, zoning out with video games, shopping, gambling, porn use, drug and alcohol use, and overeating, just to name a few. In short, the Distractor is skilled at mentally taking us out of situations that might evoke the prisoner's shame. It is often impulsive.

## THE SHUT-DOWNER

As its name implies, the Shut-Downer takes the whole system offline when it deems the situation to be too dangerous. This can happen when it believes the Warrior can't help or has failed. It takes its cue from the possum who protects itself by playing dead. The Shut-Downer pulls us out of interaction through withdrawal. Sometimes it even causes us to collapse or freeze. It believes it can't get it right and there is no escape. Depression, hopelessness, and despair are the emotions that follow. The Shut-Downer believes this withdrawal is the only way to keep us safe. The Shut-Downer whispers, "What's the point?" when the morning alarm goes off, convincing us to pull the covers back over our head. Physiologically, it highjacks our parasympathetic nervous system and drags us into the hypo-arousal state where both thinking and feeling disappear.

## JIM'S STORY

As my client Jim sat across from me, the terms of his incarceration became apparent. A highly successful executive in his early 40s, Jim seemed to have it all. He described himself as the life of the party and the envy of the neighborhood. He said everyone turned out for the parties he and his wife frequently hosted in their multi-million dollar home.

Despite appearances, Jim told me he felt like he was ruining his family. He confided his fear that others, including his family, only liked him because he was a "winner" when it came to making money. He admitted his motto since high school has been "winning is everything" and he means it. Jim said that when things don't go his way—he loses a deal at work, his soccer team underperforms, his daughter talks back—he gets angry. His Warrior seems to spring into action the minute he's not on top.

In those moments, he said he yells at his wife, reducing her to tears with his biting words. His kids face the Warrior's wrath when Jim feels disrespected. He admitted he drinks too much, his Distractor's favorite trick, to quiet the voice inside that tells him he's really a loser. When the Warrior and Distractor run out of steam, Jim said he is faced with the pain he has caused his family. He sees the hurt in their eyes and feels the eggshells on which they walk. Shame sets in—"I am a loser," he thinks. It's then his Shut-Down-er, takes over, and he locks himself in his room, sometimes staying in bed for days. Complete withdrawal.

When I asked Jim how he came to believe that winning was everything, he told me the story of his childhood. Our conversation revealed that Jim's belief of himself as a "loser" began early. His mother told him he was difficult, constantly comparing him to his "easier" older brother. His dad told him he was too sensitive and needed to toughen up. Jim said he dared to cry after his dog was hit by a car, and his father looked at him with contempt. Jim told me his dad grabbed a belt and said, "I'll give you something to cry about," and beat him so badly he had to miss school the following day. That experience convinced Jim that there really must be something wrong with him. "I really am too soft," he thought.

Jim started spending more time away from home. He found belonging when he joined the high school soccer team. He was a natural athlete and received high praise from his coaches and teammates. He was one of the best players in the region. Jim began to equate performance on the field—winning—with belonging. Winning meant love. Winning meant other guys wanted to be his friend and girls wanted to date him. This belonging motivated him to push himself to stay on top. He imprisoned the part of him that feared his father was right and that deep down he actually was a loser.

The Warrior pushed him harder in the weight room and on the field. His drive earned him a spot on a collegiate team, where he again was rewarded for his athletic ability. His belief that "I'm only valued for my performance" was solidified when, in his junior year, he got injured and missed half the season. Suddenly the coach wasn't interested in him. Jim came back strong in his senior year, and, as expected, regained the spotlight of his coach's attention.

Is it any wonder Jim is suspicious of his worth? That he is driven to succeed at any cost? Not winning or showing sensitivity meant being ignored or beaten—neither of which contribute to a sense of belonging. Through our work, Jim begin to see how the Guards who were trying to ensure connection with others were actually pushing them away. He was ready to make a change.

For me, Shut-Down-er and Perfection worked in tandem to try to shield me from the shame of my imperfection. I didn't realize how early this strategy was learned until recently when I was sorting though some old papers and came across my kindergarten report card. It was in a box of pictures that were so old that Kodak still printed the dates on the back. Mrs. A. was my teacher. Her comments were written out in flowing cursive writing—long hand—no computers. As I read it, I must confess a part of me thought she would say what a wonderful and intelligent child I was. That somehow she would be able to erase the story I had in my head of myself as invisible and not enough.

Instead, next to a slew of "Satisfactories" she wrote, "Angie drags her feet. One foot turns in. She is hyperactive. Angie moves too fast. She needs to slow down in her work. She wants to run instead of walk. Perhaps you could try actually walking with her. She needs to keep her hands to herself. She rushes through her work and makes careless mistakes; she is always in a hurry. She always wants attention."

And just like that, the words of my kindergarten teacher transported me back into the sense of shame and "too much" that I felt at age five. I heard my Critic saying, "Silly girl. Nobody cares what you think. Nobody explains things to you because you aren't worth explaining to. You wouldn't understand. Stay quiet and move under the radar. Be pretty and appropriate, but don't demand anything. You won't get it and in fact you will be shamed for wanting it." Interestingly enough, there didn't seem to be any curiosity about what might be motivating my rush or my need for attention. Nobody connected the dots between The Event Never to Be Spoken Of, and my behavior before and after our brief exodus away from my father.

As I read further down the page of remarks, I saw an added note. It was in a different color ink, just after the bit about "Angie always wants attention." It said, "improving in this area." Slam. And just like that, I could finally see the prison with me unwittingly locked inside.

## ✿ NOTICE YOUR REACTIVE FIREFIGHTER GUARDS

Do you have a Warrior, a Distractor, a Shut-Downer, or other Firefighter Guards?

Describe:

_____

_____

_____

Under what conditions do they show up?

_____

_____

_____

## ★ LETTERS FROM THE GUARDS

Write a note to yourself from each of your Guards.

What do they want you to know?

_____

_____

_____

_____

What do they believe about the prisoners they protect?

_____

_____

## CHAPTER 3

# FINDING THE KEY

Clients come to me because they have heard the call for change. They are sick of the confines of their depression and anxiety, and tired of being sad and angry. They have used all the tricks of distraction to no avail, achieving temporary relief at best. The shame hiding with the prisoner resurfaces, just beneath the hangover on Sunday morning. Clients reveal their deep sense of not belonging, not being understood, not feeling connected. This deep longing for connection continues well beyond our childhood years because, as you have learned, after our physical growth is complete, we continue to need connection for our emotional and spiritual development. We long for it because we've experienced it before. We can't long for something we've never known. That's why I love the word "remember"—because it literally means to come back into membership. For a proper jailbreak, this remembering and reconnecting are key.

There are three planes of connection, avenues for soothing the longing we feel: me to God, me to you, me to me. Let me explain. The first is transcendent. In the transcendent plane of connection, we are connected back to our Source. We relax into the remembering of being part of the Whole before we came into this life. From a spiritual perspective this can mean God or the Divine. From the view of quantum physics, this is called the Field. Whatever we choose to call it, we can relax back into being held by something bigger. Our thoughts slow, and our body opens. All is well.

The second plane of connection is interpersonal—meaning person to person. This is the one we usually think about when it comes to connection. On this plane, we connect with each other in an attempt to feel understood and known; to feel like someone has our back and we are safe. It begins with the parent-child connection, and morphs into friend and romantic connections.

The third plane of connection is intrapersonal, which simply means my connection to myself. I think of this as my connection to my wise heart. From this place, I can observe the multiplicity that is my mind, fully connecting with all the parts of me—the ones that are free as well as those that are imprisoned. I can hear the stories and soothe the pain of those incarcerated. I can help them see they aren't alone—my wise heart is always available.

For me, this intrapersonal place is sacred. It's accessed through the area around the heart, not through the head. Thus, at any given moment, we are actually able to find the sense of belonging and secure attachment—of remembering. In other words, we always have access to the key that will free us.

## SARA'S STORY

We can long for connection on these three planes, but we often don't allow it in. Sometimes we don't even recognize it when it arrives. It's hard to see it from behind bars. I was reminded of this recently when I was sitting with Sarah, a new client. Although she had an impressive day job with a fancy title at a major corporation, Sarah came to see me because, in her words, something was missing. Despite her outward success, she felt empty. She told me she was constantly trying to fill the void, striving to feel whole, to feel enough. She recited her resume with a combination of pride and embarrassment. It included dozens of meditation retreats with all the top name teachers. It included certification as a yoga instructor and hours of online self-help and spiritual workshops. She'd read dozens of books, and even experimented with psychedelic drugs in her search for nirvana. She'd done it all. Exhausted and defeated, she ended up with me.

As she talked, (and talked and talked), it was clear she was trying to convince herself (and me) that she was "enough." As she talked about her life, it was also clear that in her family, belonging and enough-ness were only conferred with great achievement. As a child, this meant perfect grades, awards and scholarships, and leadership roles. As an adult, it meant earning placement in the best university and then starting a career at a Fortune 500 company. She climbed the corporate ladder until she was at the very top. Prestige. Money. Power. She had it all and yet she was still questioning herself. Still feeling empty.

As she sat in my office, describing to me all that she knows and how much she has figured out, a part of me was thinking that I could really help her if she would only slow down and listen for a minute. I tried to interrupt a few times, but to no avail so I sat back and waited patiently. I knew Sarah needed to talk until she felt safe with me. I knew that when she felt safe, she could allow herself to be vulnerable. She could stop trying to impress me and start opening to connection. I sat and attuned to her emotional experience. I had to come alongside her, to feel her franticness and the pain beneath it, to understand the intensity of her experience. I knew that only when Sarah felt like I was truly in it with her, would she be willing to let me guide her out of it. I was patient because I know that attunement takes time. I waited patiently because I remember how hard it can be to imagine something you've never had. There's no pattern of experience to match against.

Like Sarah, we can all fall into the trap of looking outside of ourselves for the answer. After all, our first models of connections were outside of ourselves—interpersonally—with our caregivers. It often doesn't occur to us that the void we feel could be healed from within (intrapersonally). We are guilty of both seeking meaning and peace and then making them impossible to find because we can't get out of our head and into our heart long enough listen to ourselves about what we actually need—what is true for us.

Even if we do manage to listen to ourselves, we often don't trust the answer when it comes. We dismiss it as too hard (or too easy!) or illogical. We fear we will be ridiculed by others if we listen. We can't allow true knowing because true knowing isn't found outside ourselves, or even in our heads. It comes through the heart. When I refer to the heart in this sense, I am referring to the heart as both a physical organ and as portal to the more spiritual aspects our ourselves. The heart is the key.

There is an old Hindu legend cited from the Vedic tradition that begins with a time when humans had full access to the divine. Seems we humans abused our divinity (shocking, I know), and the chief of the gods decided to take it away from us. He called in a panel of advisors to discuss where it should be hidden.

"Hide it up on the highest mountain," said one.

"Bury it deep within the earth," said another.

"Put it at the bottom of the ocean," said a third.

All three ideas were dismissed because the chief was sure the humans would hunt endlessly out in the world for it, not ceasing until they possessed it again. In the end, it was decided to hide the divinity deep within the center of their own hearts, a place the chief was convinced the humans would never look. And so it was. The chief was right. And, ever since, humans have looked high and low outside of themselves for the very thing they have possessed inside all along.

## THE SCIENCE

Entrance to the experience of connection we seek can be accessed through the heart. We have to be in our body before we can launch a proper jailbreak because it is the mind itself that keeps us trapped. The mind houses the Guards and the prisoners. Why the heart? From a physical perspective, the heart is the first organ to develop in the womb. From a spiritual perspective, the heart is the place where the divine spark enters and we become human. From either perspective, the heart is where it begins—it holds the key.

A summary of research published by the Heart Math Institute (HMI) reveals that, from a purely physiological perspective, the heart has the most powerful electromagnetic field in the body. Its charge is literally measurable. It has more juice than the brain. In fact, the heart actually has its own kind of brain, evidenced by the presence of ganglia, neurotransmitters, and proteins similar to those found in the brain. Interestingly, HMI research reveals that this allows the heart to operate separately, independently, of the head. Further, it turns out that the heart is actually sending more information up to the head and to the rest of the body than is the head.[1] Seems the head isn't really in charge after all. Mind blown, huh?

When we are taking our guidance from the heart, rather than the head, we can have a different emotional experience. It's a calm, connected, peaceful state that meditators have known about for centuries. The HMI researchers call this state "heart coherence." This coherence is measured by something called "heart rate variability," which is defined as the interval between heartbeats. Heart rate variability is a measure of how the vagus nerve is operating (if you remembered that the vagus nerve is the 10th cranial nerve you read about earlier, you win!). Research reveals that the heart's rhythm sets the emotional tone for the whole system. When it is out of a flowing rhythm, in other words, when it is choppy, our mood follows. When it's smooth, our mood follows. In fact, negative emotional states are correlated with irregularities in heart rate variability, and positive emotional states with more regularity.

Dick Schwartz, founder of Internal Family Systems (IFS) therapy, describes this state of coherence as "Self."[2] I think of it as the wise heart. It is that place of calm, compassion, and courage we all have access to when we are tuned in. This essence is evident is most spiritual traditions, including Christianity's Holy Spirit, Hindu's Atman, Buddha Nature, and the Tao in Taoism, to name a few.[3]

Why does this matter? Because this business of truly living is a partnership between the divine Self and human. The wise heart inspires; humans make it happen. When they are working together, the path is clear. When the Guards are running the show without guidance from the wise heart, the prisoners remain confined, blocked from meaningful connection. One of my favorite quotes, attributed to Einstein, states: "The intuitive mind is a sacred gift and the rational mind is a faithful servant. We have created a society that honors the servant and has forgotten the gift."

When we access our wise heart, we can have compassion for all our Guards and what they protect. From this place, we can witness the Guards' stories of how they came to be and what they are protecting. We can gain the Guards' trust and be granted visitation to the inmate with the intention of healing it. This healing, described in the next chapter, is the ultimate rehabilitation that frees up both the prisoners and the Guards up to get on with the business of truly living a creative and expanding life.

Living outside this prison can be thought of as living in the zone or being in the groove. Dr. Mihaly Csikszentmihalyi (say that three times fast!), calls this "flow."[4] A professor at the University of Chicago, Csikszentmihalyi spent his career researching happiness and creativity. His work suggests that people are happiest when they are in state of "flow," which he describes as being absorbed in complete concentration on the task or situation at hand. In this state, all thoughts of self, time, and other disappear. Flow occurs when we are focused on something that is challenging enough to keep us interested, but not so out of reach that we give up. It's the ultimate in intrinsic motivation—doing something because you want to for you, not in search of some external validation. In flow, our Guards have gotten on board to make our vision a reality. We're not sneaking past them, they have opened the door. We stop thinking. We are just doing. No resistance.

So, if we are intellectual people, truly intelligent folks, why wouldn't we tune into our heart space first? Why wouldn't we want to access this heart coherence and flow state? Why wouldn't we want to access our wise heart? Why do we insist on treating it as an afterthought rather than the epicenter of our world? I think it's because we just didn't know about it. Or, we actually knew about it intellectually, but never actually experienced it. We didn't know how to get there. We had no map. No guide. Our early experiences and subsequent beliefs keep us stuck, focused externally, convinced that life had to be a struggle. The truth is for many of us it was a struggle, but it doesn't have to be any more.

How do we actually tune into our heart space? Again, both spiritual traditions and science provide a map. There are literally thousands of books you can read, retreats you can attend, and classes you can take, but the bottom line is this: you need to control your state of focus. Focused attention is your superpower. It allows you to decide what you will pay attention to. It's the difference between listening to whatever radio station happens to be playing when you turn it on or intentionally deciding which station you want to hear. One makes us passive recipients; the other makes us active, co-creators of our experience.

## SLOWING DOWN

We can't contemplate doing something different until we realize we are stuck. The key to the contemplation stage is actually slowing down. It's giving ourselves enough space to really notice what is going on inside of us rather than reacting to what's

going on outside of us. I give my clients the acronym "S.T.F.D."
Get it? They usually figure it out after a second or two. Slow.
The. Fuck. Down. I'm making refrigerator magnets. I think they
will be a great reminder.

But how do we actually slow down in those moments when
our Guards are convinced it's not safe?

I use the following exercises with my clients. The first one
triggers the parasympathetic nervous system, a.k.a., the brakes.
I learned about the importance of breath from Amy Weintraub,
founder of LifeForce Yoga.[5] This particular exercise allows us
to become calm, relaxed, and open—ready for creativity and
exploration. I'll explain more on the science after you try it. The
second exercise primes our focus. It helps us to pay attention on
purpose, to get curious, to use our superpower. Again, I'll give
an explanation after your exploration.

Another way to get focused (and thus get back into present
conscious awareness), is to simply look around the room you are in
and use your five senses to name what is perceived (sight, sound,
touch, smell, and taste). Try the next three exercises to do this.

**YOUR TURN**

## 🔐 4x4x6 BREATHING

In this type of breathing, you simply:

Inhale deeply down into your belly for the count of four. This isn't the time to flaunt your abs—let the air fill your belly so it sticks out.

Retain or hold the in breath for four counts.

Exhale for the count of six, forcing all of the air out of your lungs so that your belly button feels like it is pressed up against your spine.

Repeat for 60-90 seconds.

Try it. (Seriously, stop reading and do it now.)

What do you notice? Most people report feeling like they are less frantic, less pressured, more calm. Their thoughts are slower, and their breath is easier. They also report feeling more openness in their body—less tension all over. This sets them up to focus on the next step.

**How do you feel?**

_____

_____

_____

_____

_____

_____

## ♪ SENSING IN PRESENT TIME

Start by naming five things you see. *For example, I see the chair. I see the clock. I see the sleeping dog. I see my purse on the floor. I see the painting on the wall.*

_____

Next, name four things you hear. *I hear the ticking clock. I hear traffic outside. I hear music playing in the other room. I hear the whirl of the fan.*

_____

Then, using your sense of touch, name three things you feel. *I feel the cool leather on the couch beneath me. I feel the softness of the dog's fur. I feel the texture of my pants.*

_____

Next, using your sense of smell, name two things you smell. *I smell coffee brewing in the kitchen. I smell the scent of freshly cut grass.*

_____

Finally, see if you can notice the taste in youth mouth, or even better, the taste of the beverage close at hand. *I taste the sweetness of my tea. I taste the peppermint of my toothpaste.*

_____

Get the idea? Noticing and naming via your senses brings you back into present time because you have to actually be in present time to do this. You can't be lost in thought and connected in your body at the same time. **This practice begins by turning your head 180 degrees to the right.**

**YOUR TURN**

## ♀ ORIENTING

Then, slowly, slowly, slowly turn you head to the left, taking in all the sights and sounds in your line of sight (it's kind of like using the panoramic picture function on your smart phone).

When you are looking 180 degrees to the left, do it again until you are back to the right side.

Repeat this several times until you release a sigh, a yawn, or other evidence of relaxation in your body.

**How do you feel?**

_____

_____

_____

_____

_____

## THE SCIENCE

How does the simple act of intentional breathing and sensing help? It turns out that when the exhalation breath is longer than the inhalation breath, the parasympathetic nervous system (a.k.a., the brakes) kicks in, sending a calming signal to the brain. This rhythm of breathing actually slows down the flow of stress hormones like cortisol and adrenalin, which in turn slows down our respiration and heart rate. The mental counting (1-2-3-4) or concentrating on one of the five senses give our brain something on which to focus. When we are focused via our senses on what is right in front of us, we are back in our body, aware of the present moment.

The idea of multi-tasking is misleading. Our brain can't hold two thoughts at the same time. It can toggle back and forth between two ideas really fast, but it can't hold both simultaneously. This means you can't be replaying what happened in the past, or fretting about what might happen in the future, and focused on the present at the same time. Thus, when you focus your attention on the sensation of breathing (expanding your belly) and the act of counting or noticing, you have focused your attention in the here and now. Same for noticing what is around you via your senses.

When this happens, the parts of our brain that shut down under stress (in the prefrontal cortex), have the opportunity to come back online. We can think again. We have space to notice what is going on in our heads. The 60-90 second break gives us the ability to notice our emotional and physical state rather than being hijacked by them. It gives us the space we need to come back to ourselves.

Stated another way, these practices bring us back into our window of tolerance, where we have conscious awareness of what we are thinking and what we are feeling. This conscious awareness allows us to assess the current situation more accurately. When our vision isn't blurred by the bars of our jail cell, we are free to choose our response.

## PAYING ATTENTION ON PURPOSE

So how do we notice what is? We have to pay attention to our thoughts. We have to tune into the part of us that is able to watch our thoughts, like the view from the SkyCam at the Super Bowl. The one that is separate from and can "see" all the action. It's our compassionate observer. It is our wise heart. This can be accessed through mindfulness.

Mindfulness, as John Kabat-Zinn likes to point out, is nothing more than paying attention on purpose to what is happening right now.[6] That's it. It's being able to direct our attention to what we want to direct it to (like picking our radio station). It's about keeping our attention where we want it to stay. It's about noticing when our attention has strayed and bringing it back to the intention of our focus. As the German biologist Karl Vogt (d. 1895) explained, "The brain secretes thoughts like the stomach secretes acid." That is just what it does. The goal of mindfulness isn't to stop thinking; rather, it is to notice that your thoughts have wandered and to redirect them back to where you want them to be.

Before we get to how to apply this idea to our own incarceration, consider this question: What draws our attention? Ever watched that great magician David Copperfield? He is a master at manipulating our attention. Pick pockets have also perfected this skill. Both have learned the limits of our brain's ability to process information and have exploited it for their own gain (or our entertainment). They know that in any given moment, it is impossible to process all the information bombarding our senses. It is through our selective attention or focus that we are able to filter out all but what we have learned is relevant to our survival. Having the ability to control our attention is liberating; the inability is imprisoning. Unfortunately, we are all too easily fooled.

In my workshops, I show a video to illustrate this trickery. It's billed as an attention and perception test.[7] The video shows two teams, one with white jerseys, the other with black jerseys. It shows them passing the ball back and forth as they weave in and out of each other on the court. The viewer is asked to count the number of times the white team passes the ball. Easy enough, right? Yes and no.

Because the teams are moving around, weaving in a circle, the viewer has to track two things: where the white team is on the court and how many times they passed the ball. Two different points of focus. While most viewers can do this, it comes at an attentional price: Our brain has to ignore some information to take in other information. We can't see it all at the same time. So here's the con: While the viewers are busy focusing on the ball and the white team, a person dressed as a gorilla enters the scene, pounds its chest, and walks through the middle of the whole passing game.

Those viewers that come up with the correct number of passes are most likely to not to have seen the gorilla at all. Seriously. A chest-thumping gorilla comes through and they miss it. Those who do see the gorilla usually don't have an accurate count of ball passes. It's a trade-off. What we pay attention to is what we see. It's technically referred to as "inattentional blindness for dynamic events."[8] Google "The Monkey Business Illusion" and run your own experiment with your friends. Good times.

Here's another example. Take a look at the picture below.[9] What do you see?

Most people can see two faces. One is young woman's profile, her neck and jawline visible. The other is an old woman with a prominent nose and a pointy chin. She's wearing a head scarf. Can you see them? If you are having trouble, imagine that the young woman's chin is the old lady's nose. Which did you see first? How hard was it to shift your focus and see the other?

Interestingly, most people can see both but not right away (unless of course you have seen this picture 100 times before, in which case, you already knew the answer and probably pulled "young woman" and "old woman" answer out of your memory file without actually taking in the picture at all). This is a great example of how shifts in your attention change what you actually see. It is also another great example of how you can't hold both images (i.e., points of focus) at the same time. You were able to toggle back and forth between both images because (hopefully) in this moment, you are feeling relatively safe—safe enough to open yourself up to new learning. If you are comprehending these words, following along, you are open and receptive. You feel safe.

When you aren't feeling safe, your ability to perceive what's going on around you changes. Although we have mostly evolved out of acute states of immediate danger (we aren't being chased on a regular basis by a tiger), our brain can't tell the difference between a real threat (tiger) or an imagined threat (paper tiger). In other words, our body can respond as though the paper tiger is real. In these moments of high stress, our body is flooded with stress hormones. Blood is shunted away from the brain and visceral organs to the arms and legs, readying us to strike out or to run. Our thinking brain literally shuts down. Some people experience the sensation of tunnel vision (e.g., narrowed focus).

Recall that our nervous system is highly influenced by our emotional state and our emotional state, and the hormones associated with them, dictates the actions we take. For example, anger evokes assertion or defending while sadness leads to seeking support or withdrawing. Excitement causes us to attend and explore, while shame makes us hide and avoid. Fear causes us to fight, freeze or submit, while joy pushes us to connect and engage.

Emotions and behavior are exquisitely linked. It's important to realize that our emotions are also connected to the story or meaning we make of the situation. Remember my fated acorn hit at the softball game? The story is driven by what we are able to perceive and what we are able to perceive is what we are conditioned to see. *In other words, we tend to see what matches the patterns of experiences we've already had.* This is how we stay stuck in a repetitive pattern. If I am convinced that the kid threw an acorn at my head on purpose, I am more likely to "read" contempt on the face of the kid who is running away from the scene. If I think it was just a squirrel, I have no reaction.

For us to operate optimally in the world, our perceptions better be clear. Otherwise the whole system is misfiring. The problem is that when we are behind bars, our perceptions aren't clear. The signal gets lost or jumbled. It's kind of like what happens to the satellite radio signal when you go into a concrete parking garage or to your cell phone signal when you go through the mountains.

So how do we begin to notice what is? Once the system has been calmed with some breathing and grounding, we can get to work. Try the following exercises for yourself.

# ⚡ SCUBA SITTING

I introduce my clients to a mindfulness/paying attention on purpose exercise called Scuba Sitting.

Imagine that you are sitting at the bottom of the ocean. You can breathe just fine (hey, it's imagined). You are relaxed and calm—no place to be and nothing to do except observe.

Image that as you sit there, different sea creatures pass by. You may notice a yellow fish—and you say to yourself, "yellow fish" and you watch it swim by. A beautiful blue fish comes into your line of sight—you notice it and watch it swim away. A jelly fish floats by, you name it, and watch it go. At some point, an octopus glides by. You say "octopus" to yourself and watch it swim away. At no time do you try to catch them, nor do you try to avoid them. You just notice and name each one as it passes.

Imagine that our thoughts are like those sea creatures. In this mindfulness exercise, we practice noticing and naming what we see arise in us. We might notice an anxious thought. We say to ourselves, "there's anxiety" and we watch it rise and fall. We may notice a critical thought. We say "there's my Critic," and we notice it as it marches through.

Like noticing the cobalt blue on the fish and the darting way it swims, we can become familiar with the signature of each Guard—what each looks like, feels like and sounds like. We become acquainted with the Guards, noticing that we are separate from them. Later we will actually interact with the Guards (but not yet).

Try this practice. Start by doing it for five minutes. See if you can notice the presence of the Guards. Watch them from a place of calmness and curiosity.

**YOUR TURN**

## ♟ HEART COHERENCE

The HMI suggests the practice called "Quick Coherence Technique." It combines breathing and focused attention. I use it daily.

**The first step is Heart-Focused Breathing.**

Imagine that your breath is flowing in and out from the area around your heart. This requires focusing your attention on your chest rather than on the thoughts in your head.

Inhale for the count of five and exhale for the count of five, all the while visualizing the breath coming in and out of your heart. This balanced breathing begins to calm your nervous system, balancing the sympathetic and parasympathetic branches.

**The second step is reaching for a positive feeling.**

Reach for a positive feeling. This can be done by recalling the joy you feel when your dog wags his tail at your arrival home, the giggles of your children, the bliss of that first sip of coffee in the morning, the sound of the cardinal in the tree outside, or the sound of your daughter singing in the shower. It's something you appreciate or have gratitude for. Really try to embody the positive feeling state while you are breathing through your heart. In other words, imagine seeing the image, smelling the smells, feeling the textures, and hearing the sounds.

Continue for several minutes, all the while feeling the breath coming in and out through the heart.

**Reflections**

_____

_____

What does it feel like when we are in the coherent state? Dick Schwartz, founder of IFS, describes the state using eight "C" words: calmness, curiosity, clarity, compassion, confidence, courage, creativity, and connectedness. Quite a list! It's important to notice the experience of being in that energetic state—learning to recognize what it feels like for you. For example, when I am in that state, my shoulders relax down, my breath becomes slower and deeper, and it literally feels like there is more space in my chest. My mind slows down and I feel content. I'm not in a hurry—I'm floating along in the present. A smile plays at my mouth. I hear a slight hum in my ear and the palms of my hands and feet tingle.

I asked a couple of my colleagues about their experience of this energy. One said, "My whole body slows down and my voice softens. I literally feel my heart expanding and there is a lightness in my chest. Often I find my hands open to receive. I have neither an urge to move towards, nor away. Contentment. Next level is tingling."

Another said "I feel like I'm looking out at the world from behind my eyes. And I feel like it's a sun in me that is doing the looking. I feel a sense of calm. Everything slows down."

The experience is real people. Give it a go.

**YOUR TURN**

## ♟ HEART COHERENCE DESCRIPTION

**When I'm in this state I notice:**

My thoughts: *[e.g. slow down]*

_____

_____

_____

_____

My body: *[e.g. a smile on my face; more space in my chest; tingling in my hands]*

_____

_____

_____

_____

For the record, Sarah did eventually stop talking. Over time she let me into her vulnerability. She let me guide her back to her heart space where she finally heard what was true for her, without regard for what others thought. Moreover, she learned to use her heart—rather than her logic—as her primary guidance system. To be clear, Sarah still loves to strive. The difference is that now the striving is to fill her curiosity, not her emptiness. It's the difference between being chased and running toward. This kind of striving is energizing. Striving from a place of emptiness is exhausting.

## ★ LETTER FROM YOUR WISE HEART

Write a letter to yourself from your wise heart. It's best to do this right after you have completed the heart coherence exercise. Here's how it could start:

Dear You,

I am your Wise Heart. Here is what I want you to know...

_____

_____

_____

_____

_____

_____

_____

_____

_____

_____

_____

_____

_____

_____

_____

## CHAPTER 4

# BREAKING OUT

If you've made it this far in the book, I'm guessing you have decided to break out of your own invisible prison. The notion of "decide" may seem obvious. In reality it often isn't. This is because when we are caught behind the wall of negative beliefs, we buy into the story that there is no way our life could be any different than it is. That we are fated to stay small, sad, angry, and stuck. We believe that change is impossible. While this can seem sad to some, it can also be an ironic salve to others. If we can't make a decision, we can't be held responsible for what happens. We can't be blamed. We don't have to face the sting of failure because we never got in the game. But, as the saying goes, you can't win if you don't play. When inaction is the norm, we fall into the trap of mistaking familiar (i.e., "this is how it has always been") for comfortable (i.e., "this feels nice"). We are strangely comforted by familiar, even if familiar is actually quite uncomfortable and leads to "nothing."

So back to deciding. We have to decide we want change, that we want something as opposed to nothing. With this decision, we become willing to explore the unknown because we are completely bored or exasperated, or just plain sick of the familiar.

The jail cell has become intolerable. This longing for connection and freedom leads us back to our heart.

## STAGES OF CHANGE

Deciding and actually doing are of course two different things. According to researchers, there are five definable stages between deciding and doing.[1] The first stage in deciding is called "pre-contemplation." In this stage our response to the question of "do you want to change" is a solid NO. We aren't even considering it. In precontemplation, we might not even be aware there is a problem. We don't see the bars of our own jail cell or feel their constriction. It doesn't occur to us that our life could be any different than it already is. The way we show up in the world is familiar. This is just how it is. It's who we are. We know the routine. Why would we ever leave? Where would we even go?

The second stage is called "contemplation." In this stage our hard NO changes to a MAYBE. We start to become aware of the walls and their bars. The cell is getting a bit stuffy. We begin to consider the notion that there may be a different way to live--a floor plan that is different from what we have experienced so far. In the contemplation stage, while we are not yet committed to the escape, we are starting to consider the possibility. The walls are coming into focus for what they really are: limiting. We begin to realize that we can't be confined and creative at the same time. We long to stretch and grow.

The third stage is "preparation." and marks the shift to a solid commitment to escape. We are motivated to change. We begin to examine the blueprint of the prison in earnest. We pour over the plans and assemble our toolkit. We allow ourselves to imagine a different way of showing up in the world. We've silenced the internal voices that tell us it could never be different. We start to believe we actually could be in charge of our own lives.

"Action" is the fourth stage in deciding. The pickaxe is sharpened and demolition has begun. Bar by bar, brick by brick, the cell crumbles, and eventually, the light shines through. It guides us into a new direction. The bricks and bars now become the path on which we can walk out. We are paroled.

"Maintenance," the final stage, is about staying out (the final chapter of this book).

Are you ready to take action? You have the keys to unlocking your freedom, now you just need the blueprint for healing. "Jailbreak" makes it sound like we are orchestrating a violent overthrow. Images of tying up the Guards or sneaking past them might be playing in your mind. That's not how this Jailbreak is going down. Instead, this Jailbreak involves bringing the system back into balance by getting rid of the prison altogether. Everyone inside gets to take on a new role in service of who we want to be now.

I'll start with an overview of the whole process, then I'll break it down into action steps for you to follow. First, we activate our wise heart. We get into that ventral vagal energy flow, of openness, and connection. From this place, we get to know the

Guards—I mean really get to know them. We learn how they got their jobs, what they fear would happen if they didn't do their jobs, and what they would rather be doing if their job were no longer necessary. As we get to know them, we gain compassion and understanding for them, and they begin to trust us too. They aren't the enemy any more; they are the exiled prisoners. As we form relationships with the Guards, they eventually trust us enough to give us access to the prisoners in the hopes that we can exonerate and heal them, allowing them back as valued members of our internal community. Voting rights restored.

Second, we meet with the prisoners. We befriend them, and eventually they tell us what led to their incarceration. We hear what they came to believe about themselves and the world around them. We really witness them and their stories. This witnessing begins the healing. After they've been heard, we are able to "redo" the scenes that caused such pain, either updating them about how they actually survived it, or by playing out a different ending.

Recall from Chapter 1: Foundations, the damage that can come from a lack of attunement--the false stories we can come to believe about ourselves, which then necessitates the formation of the Guards. We're going back, so to speak, to the scene of the crime and changing the meaning, and therefore the outcome. With this exoneration, the prisoner is free to become more open, curious, and playful. She's safe. Finally, we check in with the Guards to see if they witnessed this transformation. If they haven't, we show it to them so they can change out of their uniform into something more comfortable—a role that is useful for who we are now, in present time.

## ACTION 1: RECOGNIZING WHAT IS

What is the pattern in your life that is no longer serving you? Is it debilitating self-doubt like Brenda? Is it a feeling of never being lovable like Clyde? Maybe it's a belief that you are only valued for what you do, like Jim. This "what is no longer working" is what brings my clients to see me. It's what we talk about in the very first session.

You undoubtedly already have a sense of this. It's the thought or realization that pushed you to the self-help aisle of the bookstore. It's the reason you've read this far. If you're still unclear, take a look at the negative beliefs below. You were introduced to them in Chapter 2. Which ones seem to resonate?

**YOUR TURN**

### ♟ PATTERNS OF NEGATIVE BELIEF

Circle the statements that resonate with you under each section.

Inadequacy
There is something wrong with me.
I am a bad person.
I am not enough.
I am a disappointment.
I am ugly.

# ♟ PATTERNS OF NEGATIVE BELIEF  CONT.

I don't belong.
I am invisible.
I am damaged.
I am worthless.
I am a fake.

## Responsibility/Accountability

I should have done something.
I should have known better.
It's my fault.
I did something wrong.
I am incompetent.

## Safety/Vulnerability

I am not safe.
I can't trust anyone.
I can't trust my judgment.
I can't protect myself.
It's not okay to show my emotions.
I am in danger.

## Control/Choice:

I am not safe.
I am not in control.
I am powerless.
I am helpless.
I can't handle it.
I have to be perfect.
I have to please everyone.

Now that you have sense of the negative beliefs you hold, think about what you tend to do when that negative belief is active. In other words, what prison Guards spring into action? Like Jim, does the Warrior get busy when you feel disrespected or incompetent? Does Perfection take over when you feel shame like Tammy? Does the Worrywart keep you second guessing like Brenda? Does the Shut-downer take you out when you feel helpless?

## YOUR GUARDS

What Guards surround your invisible prison? Let's really get to know them. Enter through your wise heart. To this end, we employ our open curiosity (primed by the 4x4x6 breathing) and our focused attention (primed by the senses exercises) to get started. It helps to imagine your Guards as people. Think about how you recognize a person. For example, my Grandma Wilma had trademark old lady blue hair. She also had a signature sweet and antiseptic scent fueled by the combination of her favorite perfume and Lysol disinfectant. When I came through the door, without fail, she called out in her singsong voice, "Hellooooo, how are youuuuu?" It was always her opening statement. My whole body relaxed in her presence because I knew I was loved. There was no mistaking Wilma.

The goal is to learn to distinguish the different Guards and their jobs (i.e., patterned responses). It's a bit like being able to tell who is walking up the stairs, just by the sound. Do you hear the heavy footsteps of your father? Or the quick patter of your little brother? If you slow down long enough to pay attention on purpose, you will notice that the Guards are qualitatively different.

So how do you actually get to know them? Recall that you started this process back in chapter two (review if needed). Imagine you are taking the Guards (one at a time) out for coffee. Or a beer. Your choice really. The point is to hang out with them long enough to learn what makes them tick. Can you be genuinely curious about them? In other words, can you approach them with the key in your hand—openness, calm, curiosity—a sincere desire to attune? You can't meet them with any hidden agenda. They are experts at sensing ulterior motives and will refuse to open up. I encourage my clients to journal about what they learn—to describe the Guards like characters in a story. Some sketch pictures of their Guards. They may look like cartoon figures, shapes, or just colors. One client let her Guards write postcards to her: "Dear Emily, you suck. You're not smart enough. No one will ever want you,' Signed, Your Critic. Addressed to Emily @Future Unknown, The Dumps, USA.

**YOUR TURN**

## ♟ GET TO KNOW YOUR GUARDS

Here is a list to get you started. Remember, you may have different Guards, or your Guards may have different names. Get to know them!

Managers (Proactive)

Pleaser
Perfectionist
Worrywort
Critic
Logician

Firefighters (Reactive)

Warrior
Distractor
Shut-Downer

**For each Guard address the following:**

How do you feel it in or around your body? *(Hint: It may be a tingling in your arms, a tightness in your chest, a rumbling in your belly, a heaviness in your head.)*

_____

Does an image spring to mind?

_____

Does it have a shape, a color, a form?

_____

Does it have a smell?

_____

How old is it?

_____

How long has it been with you?

_____

What is each Guard's typical opening statement?

_____

**You can repeat this exercise for each of your Guards.**

_____

Here's one example of my Guards. My Warrior is very distinct. I know him well. My pet name for the Warrior is "Eleven." Physically, Eleven shows up between my eyebrows. It literally looks like the number eleven—two lines that form deep ruts. I've seen memes that refer to these as WTF lines, but I digress. Eleven arrives like a heavy weight that takes up residence in my forehead. He appears dark and jagged like a combination of a tornado and a storm cloud. He's cynical and contemptuous. I confess that I have other Guards that are afraid of him. He curses like a sailor, at both me and everyone else (not usually aloud— my Pleaser won't allow that--but internally he has a bullhorn!).

When Eleven is active, my internal world assumes a climate of darkness. In those moments I can't find the key to my freedom. Eleven screams, "Fuck you! There is no fucking key, you are only fooling yourself. Stop with the airy fairy bullshit!" (I told you he had a potty mouth.). He's been around since I was in middle school. My Shut-Down-er Guard keeps a close eye on Eleven. The Shut-Downer believes that if Eleven is allowed to say what he is really thinking there will be conflict. The Shut-Downer doesn't trust our interpersonal relationships enough to believe they could tolerate and even grow from the conflict. The Shut-Downer is convinced others won't like me if I'm less than pleasing so she silences me (Shut-Downer and Pleaser are roommates).

When the Warrior and the Shut-Downer are active at the same time, I go into a sort of functional freeze in which I disconnect from the emotions in my body, but continue to function in my daily life. To the outsider, I "look" fine. In reality, I'm in solitary confinement, even though I am walking around in the general population.

## ACTION 2: HAVING COMPASSION FOR WHAT WAS

Now that we have a sense of what is, we need to understand how it came to be. To do this, we have to continue attuning to the Guards. They need to feel seen, understood, and appreciated before they even will consider letting us approach the prisoners they've spent their career hiding away. Just as I learned with my client Sarah, relationship building and attunement take time. We can't go in with guns blazing trying to change anything. So, before you attempt to connect with the Guards, check in with yourself. Are you coming from your wise heart (self-energy)? In other words, are you genuinely calm, curious, and compassionate? Use the practices introduced in chapter three (i.e., 4x4x6 Breathing; Sensing in Present Time; Orienting; Scuba Sitting; and Heart Coherence) as needed.

When you are ready, focus on each Guard as you experienced and described it in the previous section. Let it know you are with it, present and open for connection. See if it has a sense of you there with it. Let it know who you are. Once the connection is made you can begin to deepen the relationship. The goal is to begin to understand the circumstances, events, and beliefs that brought the Guard into existence. Remember, the Guards are truly trying to help you.

# 🔒 HOW YOUR GUARDS CAME TO BE

### Conversation Starters

How long have you (the Guard) been with me?

_____

_____

What is your purpose?

_____

_____

What do you want for me?

_____

_____

What are you afraid will happen if you don't do this job?

_____

_____

How did you come to believe this?

_____

_____

Can you show me a memory that is attached to this belief?

_____

How did you learn to do this job?

_____

What prisoner(s) are you protecting?

_____

When I was able to sit with my Warrior, Eleven, he told me he gets active when I feel like I have been taken for granted, disrespected, or ignored. He loathes my invisibility. The Critic tells me I am to blame. "You should have done more, given more, or even demanded more." The Shut-Downer said she comes in when my pleas for connection go unanswered. She said I look needy. Pathetic. The Shut-Downer puts a muzzle on the Warrior. She finds him decidedly offensive. The Pleaser fixes my makeup. None of these Guards wants me to feel the prisoner's pain.

## ACTION 3: WITNESSING AND UPDATING

When the Guards feel like you understand and appreciate how hard they have worked on your behalf, they will let you see the prisoner. There very well may be more than one prisoner, so repeat this process as many times as needed. Remember, in our Jailbreak, we're not trying to sneak past the Guards. Instead, we're trying to offer them hope that the inmate can be healed, freeing up the Guards to shed their uniforms and do something else. We're actually getting their permission to go to the prisoners. No tricky business. Remember, the Guards weren't always Guards—they only put on that uniform in service of the greater good. When asked, they can usually tell you what they would prefer to be doing instead.

With the Guards' permission, you can enter the inmate's cell. Just as you did with the Guards, check the state of your heart. Are you feeling openness and any warmth for this inmate? Are you interested in its story? Are you ready to listen to it without interruption, without trying to fix it or tell it why it's mistaken? Listening with an open heart is a tall order, but if you have been practicing the exercises in Chapter 3, I have every confidence you can do this. Keep practicing.

The goal is to get to know the prisoner as you did the Guards. Where do you feel it in or around your body? Is it an aching in your chest? A rock in your stomach? A sadness behind your eyes? Does an image come with it? Once you have a sense of it, let it know you are there with it. Let it know it is no longer alone. Be patient. Prisoners aren't used to visitors. It may be wary. It may be angry. It may ignore you. As shame researcher Brene Brown says, "Not everyone has earned the right to hear your story."

Earn the right to hear its story. Stay open. Stay curious. Be patient. I remind my clients that witnessing a prisoner is a lot like interacting with a hurt child or a frustrated partner. Going into lecture fix-it mode with either isn't helpful. In fact, it usually shuts the conversation down. I encourage my clients to come alongside the child or partner in attunement. It's only when others feel seen and truly understood that they are open to input from you.

As previously mentioned, when we are outside our window of tolerance, the thinking part of our brain is unavailable. In other words, in those moments your child or partner can't hear the brilliant advice you are giving, even if they want to. Same goes for the prisoner. Wait. Listen to understand rather than to fix. This will take as long as it takes. With some of my clients it takes one session. For others it takes many. Be willing to go slow-- this is tender territory. If you become overwhelmed, set it aside for a while. If needed, enlist the help of a trained therapist.

Remember, prisoners usually haven't experienced the kind of attunement that would help them make adaptive sense of their experiences. That's precisely what landed them in jail. They assume whatever happened was all their fault. They weren't aware of what was going on with everyone else. Like Clyde, they assume their mother is angry because they are bad. They have no idea that she is angry because dad wants a divorce. Once the prisoners feel understood, we can begin to help them make sense of their experience in a different way. Our job in this phase of the jailbreak is to help them understand the whole story, which often changes the belief and story that was attached to it.

## ALLEN'S STORY

My client Allen and I got to know one of his prisoners in our last session. Allen, age 52, said he had been worrying all week about an interaction with someone in his social group. He said he felt like he had been rejected by this person because he hadn't been invited to his neighborhood party. Allen admitted he was frustrated with this sense of rejection because, in his words, "I didn't even really like the guy." He sheepishly acknowledged that he wanted to be the one to do the rejecting—not the other way around. He said logically he knew his sense of rejection was ridiculous, but he couldn't shake it. I asked Allen if his Logician would allow us to get to know the part that felt rejected. The Logician agreed. When it relaxed back, Allen was face to face with the prisoner.

The prisoner turned out to be a nine-year-old boy. He called him "the little one." The image was of him in third grade. The boy sat in his cell with a look of sadness and defeat. He showed Allen memories of times he felt rejected. The little boy reminded Allen of when his older brothers snuck out of the house to avoid playing with him. He showed Allen scenes of his mother telling him he was too needy, as she pushed him away. He showed him another time when the third grade bully humiliated him in front of everyone, calling him a weirdo and refusing to let him sit at the lunch table. The little one solemnly said to Allen, "There must be something really wrong with me." He continued with a scene from math class in which he was the butt of every joke. The little one told Allen he was convinced Allen was fundamentally different from everyone else—that who he actually is is disgusting and needs to be hidden. He would never fit in. Allen listened carefully, allowing himself to touch into the emotions the little one was describing. His eyes filled with tears as he relayed this interaction to me.

When the little one was finished and felt like Allen understood, he was open to hearing from Allen. Allen asked him what he needed from those around him at the time—what he wished his experience could have been. The little one thought for a minute and replied: "I needed someone to tell me I wasn't disgusting and weird. I needed someone to help me understand what was happening."

In that moment, Allen became the person the little one needed back then. Allen told him he was a beautiful child. He told the little one that he was an observant child, hungry for information and connection. He said his family couldn't give it to him because they had their own issues. He told the little one that his mother suffered from depression and didn't connect with anyone. She actually loved him but was in such pain she couldn't show him. He told the boy that his dad raged at everyone because he had been abused by his father, not because he hated the little one.

Allen reminded him that he was six years younger than his brothers and they were just trying to escape the negativity of home. It wasn't personal. He told the little one he sometimes overwhelmed others in his attempts to make friends, but that was only because he was starved for connection at home and just didn't know how to make friends. He assured the little one that there was nothing wrong with him.

Allen reminded the little one that he was part of him and that they survived that terrible time. He assured the little one he didn't need to worry about rejection anymore—that he belonged with Allen. He didn't need to stay stuck in the prison of the past. He was free to be his inquisitive, observant, joyful self. He could begin to trust that Allen always had his back. He said he was ready to release those ugly feelings and beliefs about being disgusting and weird. Together, Allen and the little one built a huge bonfire and burned up all the beliefs of himself as disgusting and weird. They replaced them with feelings of curiosity and joy.

## THE SCIENCE

Sounds like a crazy story, yes? Internal conversations, imaginary bonfires? What the heck? What happens in the brain when we go through this process of connecting with and witnessing the Guards and prisoners? Reconsolidation theory provides a clue. According to Bruce Ecker, reconsolidation describes a specific process through which synapses (i.e., connectors in the neural networks) associated with particular memories, and their accompanying thoughts, feelings, beliefs and behaviors, can be unlocked and updated with new information.[2]

I think of it as us accessing a particular software program (i.e., implicit memory) that has been minimized on the desktop of our mind. When we focus our attention on it, we maximize it into full view of our conscious awareness. We need to update it with current information, like when upgrading from Windows95 to Windows2020. We aren't scrapping the whole system, just fixing the bugs and helping it evolve to where computers are now 25 years later.

For this update to occur, the implicit memory and the associated beliefs from that memory must first be "reactivated." This happens when we focus on the prisoner (remember, focus as our superpower to help neurons fire together and then wire together), and begin to attune to it. In this case, attunement means connecting to the emotional experience, not just listening to the words.

Remember the tears in Allen's eyes? Ecker's research reveals that the chemical signature of emotion makes the implicit memory malleable—open for updating. Emotions are actually a key component to memory formation. Those experiences that evoke strong emotion grab our attention and are coded quickly. For example, you don't have to touch a hot stove more than once to learn (i.e. form a memory) not to do it again.

The second step of this reconsolidation process occurs with the update, or addition of a coherent narrative provided by an attuned other. This update directly contradicts the information (the story) that is currently in the memory file. For Allen, the belief that he was ignored as a child because there was something wrong with him was contrasted with the idea that it was actually misattunement from his parents.

So emotion opens the memory, contradictory information is introduced, and the memory is updated. Because the memory itself is altered, the associated strategies (i.e., the Guards) that developed around the memory are no longer triggered, and thus the strategies are not needed. When this happens, they are free to assume a role in the system that is helpful today.

## THE POWER OF CONNECTION

Research on interpersonal relationships is clear on the positive power of connection. For example, in his famous "hand holding" study, Dr. Jim Coan, associate professor of neuroscience at the University of Virginia, used brain imaging to track levels of threat response in the brains of study participants under three different experimental conditions. In all three, the participants were immobilized in an fMRI (functional magnetic resonance machine), waiting for an electrical shock (the "threat" in the experiment).

In the first condition, the participants were alone. In the second, the participants were holding the hand of a stranger (the research assistant). In the third, the participants were holding the hand of their romantic partner. Not surprisingly, those holding someone else's hands showed significant decreases in their threat response--those holding the hand of a loved one most of all.[3]

Other researchers have demonstrated that our perception of the difficulty of a situation literally changes based on the degree of social support we have. In one study, researchers asked hikers, either alone, or with friends, to rate the steepness of the slope of the hill they were about to climb. Findings revealed that those who had social support (i.e., they were hiking with a friend) rated the hill as less steep than those hiking alone.[4]

I believe the process of getting to know the Guards and witnessing the prisoners works in the same way. Although it's operating intrapersonally, this process helps our parts to feel connected. In other words, our parts realize they're not in it alone (even if there aren't actually people around us!). We are actually attuning to our own internal world, helping our parts have secure attachment to our wise heart (or Self). When we feel this internal secure attachment, it, like external social support, allows our nervous system to shift into the ventral vagal portion of the parasympathetic response. This calm, connected, curious, and creative state is necessary for us to grow. From this place, our wise heart is in the lead, and our parts can get on board to follow its direction. You'll read more about this in the final chapter.

---

**YOUR TURN**

### ♟ GET TO KNOW YOUR PRISONERS

It's time to get to know your prisoners. Remember, you can pause this exercise at any time and come back to it later. We're trying to keep you within your window of tolerance as you embark on this next healing step.

Where do you feel the inmate in or around your body?

_____

What does it look like?

_____

Is your heart open to it?

_____

Can it sense your presence?

_____

Attune to it until it does. Sent it warmth until it sees you. **Let it know who you are and that you are here for it.**

# ♟ HOW YOUR PRISONER CAME TO BE

**Ask the prisoner to tell you how it came to be incarcerated.**

What are the images, sensations, beliefs, and thoughts around this? Really listen until it feels understood. Don't interrupt to update it yet.

_____

_____

_____

Ask it what it needed to have happen instead. If it doesn't know, give it some suggestions. It may be that you go back as an adult and intervene on its behalf.

_____

_____

_____

_____

Replay the scene(s)--giving the inmate the support that it didn't have then.

_____

_____

_____

_____

**When done properly, you will feel this in your body. It's not a cognitive exercise.**

**YOUR TURN**

## 👤 UPDATE AND UNBURDEN

From the vantage point of who you are now, help the prisoner understand why what happened back then.

Using language that is developmentally appropriate for its age, let the prisoner know of the larger context that was operating outside its awareness.

_____

_____

_____

Help it release the negative beliefs it developed. Let it know it doesn't have to hold onto it anymore. If it's ready, ask it how it wants to let it go. It may want to release it to the wind, bury in the earth, throw it in the ocean, or burn it up in a fire. Ask it. It will know what it wants. Then help it make it happen in your mind's eye.

_____

_____

_____

Ask the inmate if it wants to leave that scene and come to present time with you.

_____

_____

_____

Let it know you can protect it now. Bad thing over. Safety restored.

When this process is complete, it doesn't mean we will never be triggered again; rather it means we have more conscious awareness of our internal experience. This awareness allows us to choose our response rather than simply reacting as usual. Here's a recent example from my life.

About a month ago, I got an email from a fellow therapist. Let's call her Karen, though that's not her real name. Karen is a well-respected therapist in the area. I got to know her better when she took one of the workshops I taught for therapists about IFS. I really like and respect her. The subject line of Karen's email said simply: Assistance? (Beg). Karen asked if I could treat a dear friend of hers who was going through a particularly difficult time. I could tell by the tone of the email that Karen was scared. She wanted me to see this person daily for several weeks in an effort to get her stabilized, then multiple times a week thereafter. She was willing to pay for all of it. Karen's message felt a bit like the scene in the first Star Wars movie where R2D2 plays the video message on repeat of Princess Leah asking Obi Wan Kenobi for help: "Help me Obi Wan, you're my only hope." It felt that dire.

As I read the message, I could feel my internal system getting activated. My first reaction was, "Of course—she's desperate and I have to help!" This was my Pleaser (I'm pretty sure the Pleaser showed me the Star Wars scene!). The Pleaser listed the litany of reasons I had to take on a new client: "You are a good therapist and you can help. Karen's a colleague. She took your class. She respects you. She's a big deal in the therapy community. She will be angry if you don't help her. She might tell everyone you are a terrible person" and so on and so on.

In short, the Pleaser was responding to the old fear of the former inmate—the younger me that feared that if she didn't please everyone she would be alone. I felt pressure to respond immediately, to leap into action to prove my worth.

At this point, one of my managers stepped in. "You can't do this," she said. "Your schedule is already well over capacity. You are already close to burn out. You will be resentful if you take this on."

I felt caught between the two of them.

At this point, I did what I tell my clients to do: slow the fuck down. S.T.F.D. I took my hands off the keyboard and went for a walk. I needed to slow down so I could respond from my wise heart rather than reacting from a Guard. On the walk, I told the Pleaser that Karen may be disappointed with my response. I told the Pleaser that Karen may even tell everyone I am a horrible therapist. I let the Pleaser know I could handle it. I reminded the Pleaser that my little girl doesn't have to deal with Karen's disappointment--that the adult me can handle it. The Pleaser relaxed. I returned home and began to craft my response. Here's an excerpt:

> I am so sorry to hear about what's happening. I love
> how committed you are to helping—very generous
> of you...I so appreciate your confidence in me and

understand how vulnerable all of you must be feeling. I am afraid I can't commit to daily sessions right now—I'm also slammed and it sounds like she may need a higher level of care than I can give.

I then made specific suggestions about in-patient treatment centers and recommended a psychiatrist who could help with a medication consult. Before I hit the send button, I checked in with my system. I felt settled in my body; my wise heart was calm and certain about my response. I hit send.

**EXTRA CREDIT**

★ **CHECK-IN**

Check in with the former inmate daily for the next several weeks. This focused attention helps to solidify the new learning and connection.

## CHAPTER 5

# STAYING OUT

Congratulations! You're out on parole. But now what? When you've been living one way for so long, how do you move forward? At this point, we have the opportunity to develop a new blueprint, a new pattern. Do we want more adventure? Do we want more patience? Do we want to change how we look? When we no longer have to focus on hiding parts of ourselves, we are free to create!

## WHAT DO YOU WANT?

This question of what we want is often harder than it sounds. Clients are usually pretty clear about what they *don't* want.

"I don't want to be so angry."

"I don't want to be sad."

"I don't want to worry so much."

"I don't want to argue."

When I redirect and ask what they would like instead, I am often met with silence. For some, the lack of response comes from simply never being asked that question before. They were too preoccupied with survival.

Abraham Maslow, an American psychologist and philosopher, studied psychologically healthy people. From this work, he developed Maslow's hierarchy of needs.[1] It's of interest here because it moves us from merely surviving to actual thriving in our full potential. I don't know about you, but I want to live at my full potential!

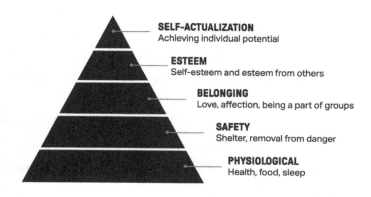

**SELF-ACTUALIZATION**
Achieving individual potential

**ESTEEM**
Self-esteem and esteem from others

**BELONGING**
Love, affection, being a part of groups

**SAFETY**
Shelter, removal from danger

**PHYSIOLOGICAL**
Health, food, sleep

The lower portion of the hierarchy lists basic survival needs starting with physiological (i.e., food, water, shelter) and then safety (i.e., physical and psychological). The next level up in the hierarchy focuses on social needs and belonging (i.e., affection and attachment), followed by esteem needs (i.e., competence/reputation).

Maslow's final level is entitled self-actualization and deals with living in our full potential. This is what we are ready for after the Jailbreak. Maslow's characteristics of self-actualized people can inspire us to think about how we want to live outside the confines our prison. For example: Can you imagine not being deterred by ambiguity and uncertain? Can you imagine accepting yourself (and all of your parts) with compassion? Can you imagine living life as a journey rather than a destination? A process rather than an outcome? Can you imagine being so comfortable with who you are (even your imperfections) that you can let others be who they are? Can you imagine feeling energized by growth, by learning? Can you imagine feeling like your life has purpose and meaning? Can you imagine not getting upset by the little things? Can you imagine being grateful for what you do have and less focused on what you lack?

Do these examples help you think about what you want? An example from my client Martie is illustrative. When we got to the parole phase of our work, I asked her want she wanted now. She replied, "I want to lose 20 pounds."

Before you say, "What's weight got to do with full-potential living?" stay with me. First, I asked Martie to describe why losing weight was important to her. Her initial response was that she would look better and be "healthy." She admitted that part of her desire was vanity—she wanted to look cute in her new workout clothes. As we probed deeper, she admitted she fears getting older and losing mobility. She feared becoming wheelchair bound as her mother had been. She said when this happened, her mother seemed to withdraw from the world.

As we talked, Martie's desire became clearer. She said she wanted to be able to play with her granddaughter. She said she even wanted to be able to dance at her granddaughter's wedding someday. I asked her to tell me how she would feel if she achieved her goal, not just how she would look or what she would do. Remember the importance of emotion in changing neural network patterns? Martie said if she had achieved this goal, she would feel better in her body—more fluid. She said would have more energy and be more vibrant. She said she would feel confident to travel on her own, looking forward to new adventures. She said she would no longer be focused on how her body was letting her down; instead, she would be proud of how well it was serving her.

Can you see how this inquiry went deeper—beyond the surface level "I should" response? After determining why this goal was important, I asked Martie to imagine what she would feel like, the emotional tone that would come with looking good in her workout clothes, having more energy, playing with her granddaughter, and traveling around the world. She imagined feeling excited, open, and tingling with possibilities. And if you felt this way (I asked) what would your impulse be? She said that she would jump out of bed and look forward to each and every day.

Free from the confines of our cell, we can begin a deeper exploration of what our heart, rather than our head, desires. We can begin to explore what is more in line with our purpose and what feeds our spirit.

Research suggests that when we imagine the sensations and the feelings that would accompany what we desire, we are actually building a new memory file in our brain, a new template, a new procedural file.[2] It's the combination of the image, and more importantly, the emotion, that comes with the image that wires the new template. In fact, brain imaging scans reveal that vivid imagining (i.e., using all five senses) truly does change the neural networks in our brain.

In an interesting study of exercise, Yue and Kelly, found that those who engaged in physical exercise increased muscle mass by 30%, while those who merely imagined exercising increased their muscle mass by 22%.[3] No kidding. In other words, we don't have to actually experience it to create a neural network of it. Peak performance coaches have used this finding for decades to train elite athletes. Professional basketball players, for example, spend as much time off the court imagining the swish of the perfect free throw as they do actually practicing the shot. Dancers "dance" their whole routine in their heads. Mental rehearsal makes them even better. What fires together wires together. Once again, it's all about where you focus your attention.

Still skeptical about the power of imagination and visualizing? Try this exercise for yourself.

## ⚡ THE POWER OF VISUALIZATION

1. Stand up and place your feet hip-width apart.

2. With your arms out like airplane wings, rotate slowly as far to the right as you can. Make a mental note of where your "wings" were pointed (i.e. notice a spot on the wall.).

3. Repeat on the other side, again making a mental note of how far you went.

**Now for the fun part!**

4. Put your arms down and close your eyes.

5. Using your imagination only, visualize yourself repeating the movement. Arms out like airplane wings (in your mind only) and turn as far right as you can. Repeat to the left (again, just in your mind).

6. Repeat two more times. Allow yourself to visualize yourself twisting slowly, just as you would if you were physically moving your arms.

7. Do the whole exercise once again, this time with your eyes open and with full physical use of your arms. Rotate to the right, and notice how far you went.

**Surprised at your progress? It's the power of visualization!!**

**Reflections**

_____

_____

**YOUR TURN**

## ☝ WHAT DO YOU WANT?

**Name what you want.** *(e.g., I want to be 20 pounds lighter; I want to have a successful career; I want to be in a loving relationship)*

_____

Visualize or run a mental movie of what it would look like if you had what you wanted. Select one "scene" or image from the movie that captures the whole experience.

Imagine what emotions you would be feeling if you got the "scene". *(e.g. calm, excited, passionate, creative, happy)*

What sensations do you notice in your body when you have the emotion attached to the scene? *(e.g., open, fluid, peaceful, relaxed)*

_____

Bring to mind the image of the scene, the associated emotion, and the physical sensation. Hold them at the same time.

While holding these three, cross your arms in front of you and slowly and rhythmically tap or pat *(left, right, left, right, etc.)* the upper part of your arm. This is called a "butterfly hug". Do this tapping 8-12 times. Notice how it deepens the experience each time you couple your focused attention with the tapping hug.

### Reflections

_____

_____

_____

## REOFFENDING

When I first thought about this book, I thought the final chapter would be about how to stay out of jail. It didn't take me long to realize that life isn't about staying out of jail. We can't truly LIVE if we are fearful of making a mistake, fearful of going back to prison. Instead, I realized this process of jailbreak is recurring. We WILL get incarcerated once again. I promise. It's inevitable. None of us is exempt. Given this reality, it makes much more sense for us to keep our toolkit handy, ready for use when we need it. In the meantime, we get to get on with the business of focusing on what we want. We realize that our sense of satisfaction comes as we pursue what we want—the pursuit puts us in that flow state that Csikszentmihalyi described.

When you get caught again, you will temporary forget all that you know about breaking out of jail. I know this from personal experience. You will get hijacked by old fears and patterns. Guards may come rushing back in with a fit of amnesia about who you have become. This can happen because you got complacent and stopped sharpening your tools. It can also happen, however, precisely because you are ready for another change. You needed a new experience to push you even further in your development. You may have to break out of other patterns of behavior that are now no longer serving you. Think of a snake shedding its skin. You have to break out again to continue growing. You have to go through it again, seeing it from a new angle, learning a new lesson. It forces you to stop, reflect, and grow.

I saw a video online of a guy who was demonstrating how to rescue yourself if you fall through the ice on a frozen pond. I grew up on a lake so I think I was compelled to watch it. What struck me was the guy's reaction when he hit the freezing water. He said something like, "At first your body will respond with shock from the cold (he paused as he gasped for breath) you won't be able to breathe." Duh, I thought. His next words were telling.

He said: "You have to wait this out—stop moving. Wait for the sensation to pass. Just wait. Only then can you get on with the business of rescuing yourself." I think this is his version of my S.T.F.D. When it comes to falling through the ice, it turns out that you can't just pull yourself up with your arms, as your first instinct might suggest. The ice around you will break. Instead, the guy said that once the shock has passed, you should start kicking your feet. The kicking builds momentum. The kicking raises your whole body to the surface. The strength of your kick eventually propels you forward, onto the intact ice. From there, you can start to inch forward, first sliding on your stomach. Then crawling. You move forward, ever so slowly and steadily, until you reach firmer ice. Only then can you stand up.

## RECAP: CALM. KICK. CRAWL. STAND.

It struck me that those are pretty good rules for a Jailbreak. We are all going to find ourselves back in the icy water or the dusty jail cell from time to time. My clients hate when I tell them that.

They want me to reassure them that nothing bad will ever happen again. They want to know they are forever cured, free from the bondage their minds create. They want a guarantee. You can imagine their initial disappointment when I drop my little truth bomb about recidivism rates.

I tell them what I am sharing with you: The only thing I can guarantee with absolute certainty is that something will trap you again. I have no idea what the trap will be; I only know that it will be. True freedom comes from knowing you know how to escape. It comes from knowing you have a blueprint. You can relax into that.

I then remind them to savor the highs of life, the times when they are feeling free, connected, and loved, because these times won't last forever. I also remind them to tolerate the lows of life's incarcerations with patience and some modicum of compassion, because they won't last forever either. Daylight follows the darkness. Darkness follows the daylight. Spring follows Winter. You get the idea. All of us need to remember that change is inevitable.

We also need to remember that we alone hold the key to our healing. Healing is actually more of an excavation, an uncovering, of something that was already there—something very valuable that was buried for safekeeping and forgotten. It reminds me of the story of the largest solid golden Buddha statue ever discovered.

The statue itself is ten and a half feet tall, weighing more than two tons. The story goes that when a war broke out in Siam (now Thailand), monks attempted to save the statute by "hiding" its true value under layers of clay. By the time they were finished covering it up, it looked like the largest mud statue of Buddha around. A sight to behold, yes, but a giant clay Buddha was of no value to the advancing soldiers. They walked right by it. The disguise worked. Unfortunately, the soldiers killed all the monks, leaving no one to recognize the treasure buried beneath the mud. The brilliance of its golden shine lay dormant for literally centuries.

In 1957, the statue was relocated to a new location. When the crane lifted it, the clay around it began to crack. A monk, concerned about the crack in the giant Buddha, examined the damage with a flashlight. Light hit the gold below and bounced back out. Bit by bit, the mud, the barrier to the statute's true brilliance, was chipped away. It took a while. It was careful work. But then the Buddha in all its glory was revealed.

So…get out there.

Live.

Follow your desire.

And break out.

As many times as needed.

You got this.

**CLASS DISMISSED.**

# ENDNOTES

## INTRODUCTION

1   Hawkley, L, & Cacioppo, J. (2010). Loneliness Matters: A Theoretical and Empirical Review of Consequences and Mechanisms. *Annals of Behavioral Medicine*, 40(2).

## CHAPTER 1 FOUNDATIONS

1   Kinsella, M., & Monk, C (2009). Impact of maternal stress, depression & anxiety on fetal neurobehavioral development. *Clinical Obstet Gynecol.*, 52(3), 425-440.

2   Montagu, A. (1988). Touching: *The Human Significance of Skin.* Harper paperbacks

3   MacLean, P.D. (1990). *The Triune Brain in Evolution: Role in Paleocerebral Functions.* Plenum, New York, N.Y.

4   Pert, C. (1997). *Molecules of Emotion: The Science Behind Mind-Body Medicine.* Scribner. New York, NY.

5   Sullivan, M.W., & Lewis, M. (2003). Emotional Expression of Young Infants and Children: A Practitioner's Primer. *Infants and Young Children*, 16(2), 120-142.

6   Wadsworth, B. J. (1971). *Piaget's Theory of Cognitive and Affective Development: Foundations of Constructivism.* Allyn &

Bacon Classics Edition.

7   Porges, S. (2011). *The Polyvagal Theory: Neurophysiological Foundations of Emotions, Attachment, Communication, and Self-regulation* (Norton Series on Interpersonal Neurobiology. Norton Press.

8   Rizzolatti, G. (2005). The Mirror Neuron System and Imitation. In S. Hurley & N. Chater (Eds.), *Perspectives on imitation: From neuroscience to social science: Vol. 1. Mechanisms of imitation and imitation in animals* (pp. 55–76). MIT Press.

9   Siegel, D. (1999). *The Developing Mind: How relationships and the brain interact to shape who we really are.* The Guilford Press, New York, NY.

10  Tronick, E. (2007) *The neurobehavioral and social-emotional development of infants and children.* W.W. Norton & Company, NY.

11  Longfellow, Henry, W. (1857). *The Complete Poetic Works of Henry Wadsworth Longfellow.* Cambridge Edition.

12  Ainsworth, M., Blehar, M., Waters, E., & Wall, S. (1978). *Patterns of Attachment.* Hillsdale, NJ: Erlbaum.

13  Benoit, D. (2004). Infant-parent attachment: Definitions, types, antecedents, measurement and outcome. *Paediatr Child Health*, 9(8): 541-545.

14  Harlow H. F., Dodsworth R. O., & Harlow M. K. (1965). Total social isolation in monkeys. *Proceedings of the National Academy of Sciences of the United States of America.* Retrieved from https://www.ncbi.nlm.nih.gov/pmc/articles/PMC285801/

pdf/pnas00159-0105.pdf

15  Bowlby, J. (1951). *Maternal care and mental health.* London: Her Majesty's Stationery Office.

16  Middlebrooks, J.S., Audage, N.C. (2008). *The Effects of Childhood Stress on Health Across the Lifespan.* Atlanta (GA): Centers for Disease Control and Prevention, National Center for Injury Prevention and Control.

17  Dr. Diane Poole Heller (2019). *The Power of Attachment: How to create deep and lasting intimate relationships.* Sounds True. https://dianepooleheller.com/attachment-test/quiz_-whats-your-attachment-style_big/#iLightbox[postimages]/0

## CHAPTER 2 GETTING STUCK

1  Hebb, D. (1949) Monograph. The organization of behavior: *A neuropsychological theory.*

2  Darius Ilgunas, Proven Strategies to Succeed at School https://www.goodreads.com/quotes/7384769-i-cnduo-t-bv-leiee-taht-i-culod-aulaclty-uesdtannrd-waht-i

3  Shapiro. F. (2001). *Eye Movement Desensitization and Reprocessing: Basic Principles, Protocols and Procedures.* Guildford Press. New York, NY.

## CHAPTER 3 FINDING THE KEY

1  Childre, D., & Martin, H. (1999). *The HeartMath Solution.* Harper Collins. San Francisco, CA.

2  Schwartz, R., & Sweezy, M. (2019). *Internal Family System*

*Therapy (2nd Edition)*. Guilford, Press, New York, NY.

3    Schwartz, R., & Falconer, R. (2017). *Many Minds, One Self: Evidence for a radical shift in paradigm.* Center for Self Leadership, Oakland, IL.

4    Csikszentmihalyi, M. (2008). Flow: *The psychology of Optimal Experience.* Harper Perennial Modern classics. NY

5    Weintraub, A. (2012). *Yoga Skills for Therapists: Effective Practices for Mood Management.* Norton. New York, NY.

6    Kabat-Zinn, J. (1990). *Full Catastrophe Living: Using the Wisdom of Your Body and Mind to Face Stress, Pain, and Illness.* Delta Books. New York, NY.

7    https://www.youtube.com/watch?v=IGQmdoK_ZfY

8    Simons D., & Chabris, C. (1999). Gorilla in our midst: Sustained inattentional blindness for dynamic events, *Perception,* 28, 1059-1074.

9    Illustration credited to Hill, W.E. 1915. *My Wife and My Mother-in-Law.* Puck. Puck Press.

## CHAPTER 4 BREAKING OUT

1    Prochaska, J. O., & DiClemente, C. C. (1982). Transtheoretical therapy: Toward a more integrative model of change. *Psychotherapy: Theory, Research & Practice,* 19(3), 276-288.

2    Ecker, B., Ticic, R., & Hulley, L. (2012). Unlocking the emotional brain: *Eliminating symptoms at their roots using memory reconsolidation.* Routledge. NY: New York.

3    Coan, J., Schaefer, H., & Davidson, R. (2006). Lending a
     Hand: Social Regulation of the Neuronal Response to Threat.
     *Psychological Science,* 17 (12) 1032-1039.

4    Schnall, S., Harber, K.,  Stefanucci, J. & Proffitt, D. (2008).
     Social support and the perception of geographical slant.
     *Journal of Experimental Social Psychology,* 44(5), 1246-1255.

## CHAPTER 5 STAYING OUT

1    Maslow, A. H. (1943). A theory of human motivation. *Psycho-
     logical Review,* 50(4), 370-396.

2    Shapiro. F. (2001). *Eye Movement Desensitization and Reprocess-
     ing: Basic Principles, Protocols and Procedures.* Guildford Press.
     New York, NY.

3    Yue, G. & Kelly, C. (1992). Strength increases from the motor
     program: Comparison of training with maximal voluntary
     and imagined muscle contraction. *Journal of Neurophysiology,*
     67(5), 1114-1123.

# ACKNOWLEDGEMENTS

While writing is a solitary endeavor, its inspiration is communal. I am grateful to so many!

## TO MY STUDENTS AND CLIENTS

Thank you for trusting me to be with you on your learning and healing journey. I have gained even more than I have given through our connection. Your courage inspires me daily.

## TO MY TEACHERS

Dick Schwartz: Thank you for creating this amazing model that has forever changed the way I live and work. Your support has been invaluable.

Sonia Choquette & Sabrina Choquette Tully: You continue to teach me to listen to the Divine and to trust my vibes. I am grateful for your clear teaching and loving support.

Dan Siegel: Thank you for bringing interpersonal neurobiology to the psychotherapy conversation and helping me to understand that we are truly wired to connect.

Amy Wientraub: I am so grateful to have met you! Thank you for teaching me the power of breath to reconnect to life and for your support and guidance in expanding my teaching reach.

Eric McCollum: You have supported and inspired me in so many ways as a colleague, mentor, and friend! Thank you for introducing me to meditation and Buddhist psychology. It marked the beginning of my transformation. And the memes are pretty cool too…

## TO MY TECHNICAL SUPPORT TEAM

Stuart Horowitz: My developmental editor and writing coach. I'm grateful the synchronicities of the universe that helped me find you. You were the perfect blend of compassionate teacher and tough love. www.BookArchitecture rocks!

Darci Allen: Copyeditor extraordinaire. Thank you for your attention to detail and unwavering support.

Jenny Johnson: My website, book cover and layout designer. You get me! I am grateful for the creativity and support of the Loom Collective. www.theloomcollective.com

Beta Readers: I am so grateful to the patient colleagues and friends who read and commented on earlier versions of this book: Chris Burris, Lauren Carter, Leigh Conant, Anna Maria Francis, Steve Gladis, Mara Hirschfeld, Sandy McMaster, Sara Platt, Susan Perkins, Carolyn Kniffin Pommerantz, Linda Rogers, Nancy Spidle, Kerry Alison Wekelo and Mary Woznysmith. Thank you for your wise counsel and attention to detail.

## TO MY TRIBE

With gratitude to my tribe of the most amazing women: Carolyn Kniffin Pomerantz, Martha Arnett, Linda Rogers, Leigh Conant, Faye Fiore, Alison Shorter-Lawrence, Sara Platt, Aggie Byers, and Judy Allen. Thank you for your unwavering belief in me and this project.

## TO MY FAMILY

Darrin: Together we've experienced the highest of highs and lowest of lows…and we're still here! You have made me want to be the best version of myself and to inspire you to do the same.

Regina & Samantha: Being your mom is truly the best thing I've ever been given the opportunity to do. You are the inspiration for my ongoing journey of healing and growth. Thank you for being my daily reminder of what matters most. Love you, love you. xoxoxoxoxo

**METTA,**

# ABOUT THE AUTHOR

Angela Huebner, Ph.D., is a licensed Marriage and Family Therapist (LMFT) in private practice in Falls Church, Virginia. She combines the art of psychotherapy with the science of change to help people identify and break out of patterned thoughts and behaviors that keep them stuck. Angela has been studying and working in the field of mental health for more than 30 years. She earned her Ph.D. in Human Development and Family Studies at the University of Arizona. For 17 years, she was a tenured associate professor in the Department of Human Development's graduate Marriage and Family Therapy Program at Virginia Tech in Falls Church, Virginia. Angela believes that when we are out of alignment with ourselves or with our partners, our system (body, mind, spirit) lets us know. Sometimes our system uses the language of depression. Sometimes worry and anxiety. Sometimes anger or sadness. Sometimes aches and pains. Our internal system provides us feedback if we listen. Angela provides just the tools we need to slow down and tune in. In addition to her clinical work, Angela provides workshops, consultation and coaching. For more information about Angela go to www.angela-huebner.com

Made in the USA
Coppell, TX
16 April 2022